In the House of Remembering

The Living Tradition of Sufi Teaching

VOLUME ONE

Praise for *In the House of Remembering*:

The thirty remarkable short lessons assembled here are fascinating exemplars of *suhba* (*sohbet*), the traditional Sufi process of "companionship": i.e., the illuminating relationship of inner conversation that links the spiritual guide and each listener, awakening the soul's unfolding remembrance of that Teacher we all share. Reading these talks, with their smoothly unfolding mix of Sufi stories, Rumi's poetry, illuminating personal experiences, and scriptural reminders, constantly feels like being in the presence of a modern-day Rumi. Those pedagogical elements may be familiar to some, but here they are infused with a palpable universality, accessibility, practical focus, comprehensiveness—and above all, with a constant, assured sense of *reality* and immediacy—that movingly reflect a lifetime of spiritual experience, commitment, and engagement with fellow journeyers from many different religions, cultures, and pathways of realization. Whatever their ostensible subject, each conversation here evokes a marvelous balance—and creative tension—between communion and community, meditation and active service, awareness of the timeless and immersion in the shared challenges of everyday life. This is truly a "bedside book," a work that will seem (and *be*) new and enlightening each time one opens it up....

~Prof. James W. Morris, Boston College, author of *The Reflective Heart*

These illuminating discourses, covering a wealth of themes relating to the inner life, open an accessible and refreshing window to the mature practical spirituality within the living tradition of Sufism. Rooted in the spontaneous guidance and connection of hearts that occurs in the healing and nurturing practice of *Sohbet*, they carry the direct, immediate and intimate voice of that quality of spoken language that is not distanced by abstraction, encumbered by complexity, or entangled in the knots of the rational mind. This is the work of an authentic teacher who helps us in sincerity and love to reflect deeply on our inner states within the concrete reality of our daily lives and by so doing to come ever closer to our longed-for awareness of Divine Unity.

~Jeremy Henzell-Thomas, essayist and former Visiting Fellow at the Centre of Islamic Studies, University of Cambridge

In the House of Remembering

The Living Tradition of Sufi Teaching

VOLUME ONE

INTRODUCTION BY MAHMOUD MOSTAFA

Kabir Helminski

Threshold Books
Escondido, London, Istanbul

Published by Threshold Books
Escondido, London, Istanbul
© 2020 All rights reserved
ISBN: 978-0-939660-40-7

Cover image; The Rumi Dome
at CalEarth, designed by Nader Khalili.

Contents

Introduction I
What Do We Need a Spiritual Path For? 1
Nothing to Fear 8
Initiation into the Inner Life 12
Unite with the Living 17
We Are the Context Not the Content 22
The Body is a Servant 28
Polishing the Heart 34
Make God Your Companion in Every State 40
Hearing the Music of Meaning 51
The Inner Ablution 54
Offering the Heart, Levels of Purification 61
Humbleness, Gratitude, Love 65
What Does it Mean to Be a Dervish? 70
Reflections on Suleyman Dede, an Ocean of Love 77
The Drop That Knows 79
Supplication: Why Certain Prayers Are Not Answered 84
The Essence of the *Hadiths* 89
The Prophet's Character: What the *Hadiths* Really Say 95
The Prophet on the Perfection of Character 99
Some Sayings of Hazrati Ali 106
Be Gold Yourself, the Seven Levels of Reality 111
How the False Self Dissolves 118
Internal and External Waystations on the Path 122
Hope, Activity, and Awe 126
Developing Will and the Nature of Attainments 131
The Inner Life: Aspects of the Heart 135
Be An Impartial Witness 142

The Word and the Name 147
Beauty as a Way of Life 156
Sustaining Progress on the Path 158

Acknowledgements

This book has come together through the efforts of many devoted friends who have helped to record, transcribe, and edit our conversations and otherwise supported this work: David Ginsberg, Norma McOmber, Kamran Sarwar, Meghan Sayres, Elizabeth Moore, Debra Shatoff, Sadat Malik, Daniel Dyer, Mahmoud Mostafa, Hamida Battla Safi Qureshey, and Donia Fahim.

Introduction

Mahmoud Mostafa

THIS BOOK is intended to take you into the heart of a living, vibrant, and contemporary Sufi community, the Threshold Mevlevi community, by giving you a taste of the spiritual teaching transmitted by the guide (*shaikh*) to the members of the community (dervishes) who are the seekers upon the Sufi path. This book contains a selection of 31 spiritual conversations (*sohbets*) lovingly transcribed in this remarkable volume. In the Mevlevi Sufi tradition, as with most Sufi schools, the *sohbet* is central to the transmission of the ancient spiritual guidance to purify the hearts and effect the inner transformation of the dervishes. I hope to share with you my own experience with the Threshold Sufi community, and to give you a brief overview of the fundamental teachings and methods of this School of Love.

Love on Mount Barakah

It was the summer of 1995. I traveled across the country from Southern California to the lush green mountains of northern Vermont. I was going to join a retreat that would change my life forever. As I drove from Burlington Airport on the two-hour-long journey to Burke Mountain where the retreat was being held, my mind was occupied with so many thoughts; "What will it be like?" I wondered. "What will I find there? What kind of people will be there? Will it be authentic or some kind of a cult? How will I know if they are for real? Am I really ready for this?"

I arrived at the retreat site which I found to be a ski school complex. It was early evening and the sun was beginning to set. As I walked in, I could see people all around the dining area finishing their dinner. They were seated in small groups in quiet conversation. Feeling uneasy and self-conscious at the gazes of the people as I entered, I headed towards the back door and, as I walked outside, I saw two men standing together talking. "Hello! Welcome. Are you here for our retreat?" the taller man with the full head of hair streaked with silver grey strands greeted me. "Yes, I am," I replied shyly.

"My name is Kabir, and this is our guest teacher from Turkey, Selim Baba," he said with a warm smile that eased my anxiety. The other man nodded, and, smiling, greeted me. "*Selamun alaykum*," he said cheerfully. I returned his greeting, "*Wa alaykumu Salaam*."[1] He was older and smaller with sharp features that indicated a keen intelligence. "Would you like something to eat? There is still plenty of food left," Kabir offered. "Thank you, I already ate. I will have some tea if it's available," I responded. "Good, let's go inside and you can meet the rest of our friends," Kabir said as he led me back into the dining hall. And so my journey into Sufism began.

Later that evening, we gathered in the Sufi circle. We were a group of about thirty people. We met in a large room, sitting upon cushions on the carpeted floor in a full circle. At the front of the room a green banner hung on the wall with golden Arabic calligraphy. It said, "O Presence of our Master Muhammad Jalaluddin Rumi, may Allah sanctify his secret."[2] The design of the calligraphy was in the shape of a turban. There were two sheepskins laid down on the floor before the banner and upon these Kabir and Selim Baba sat. The lighting in the room was soft and subdued. We started with a silent meditation focusing on our breath and silently reciting "*La ilaha il Allah*"[3] with each cycle of breath. Although I had recited this phrase countless times in my life, this was the first time for me doing it with this kind of attention. My mind wandered in every direction as thoughts flooded my consciousness. My body wouldn't stay still; I fidgeted constantly as the tension in my back and shoulders grabbed my attention. I kept trying to be still, to come back to my breath and the words I was reciting, "No god but God." Although it was difficult for me to maintain any prolonged attention, I felt warmth and tenderness in my heart. The rhythm of my breath in unison with so many others, the setting of the circle, the soft lights, the golden calligraphy on the wall, everything together seemed to

---

1. This is the greeting Muslims throughout the world give. It means "Peace be upon you," to which "And upon you Peace" is returned.
2. "*Ya Hadrati Mawlana Muhammad Jalaluddin Qaddasa Allahu Sirrahu.*"
3. This phrase means "There is no deity except God." It is the Muslim declaration of the Unity of Being.

emanate an energy that brought peace to my heart.

The meditation lasted about fifteen minutes. Then the *sohbet* started. Kabir spoke first. "*Bismillah ar-Rahman ar-Raheem.*[4] What does it mean to be a human being?" He went on to talk about the spiritual psychology of the human being consisting of the ego (*nafs*), the heart (*qalb*), and Spirit (*Ruh*), and the relationship between these three aspects of our humanness. He spoke of how the ego can be tamed by love, about how the heart is our inner capacity to receive and comprehend meaning, and how the Spirit is our inner point of direct contact with the Divine. His words flooded my heart with wonder and awe. The words resonated with the wisdom of the Qur'an in a way that I had not experienced before. It was as if he was expressing what I knew in the depth of my being. Tears welled up in my eyes frequently during his discourse.

Then Selim Baba, a Melami shaikh and retired NATO officer from Istanbul, spoke. (He was featured prominently in *Sufism and the Path of Blame* by Yannis Toussulis.) He talked about how love can transform our egos and heal our hearts. He spoke of the relationship between us and the Divine, between the human (*insan*) and God (Allah). He spoke about how Divine Love is always flowing to us, always calling us to awaken, to return to our Source. More tears welled up in my eyes. His words resounded with Qur'anic references and with prophetic traditions. Kabir and Selim Baba's discourses rushed into me with a force that felt irresistible, with overwhelming power, and at the same time it was full of love, tenderness, and familiarity. I didn't want the *sohbet* to end!

Then we did *zhikr*. I had never experienced anything like this before. We started by chanting a prayer for forgiveness. "*Istaghfirullah*,"[5] we called out over and over again in unison, our voices reverberating throughout the room. Then, to the accompaniment of large hand drums we chanted, "*La ilaha il Allah*," with rhythmic breathing and beautiful melody. Then we chanted, "*Allah, Allah, Allah*," calling out from the depths of our hearts. The beat of the drums, the resonance of our voices, the rhythm of our breath all came together to engulf us in what felt

---

4. In the Islamic tradition, we consecrate every undertaking by invoking this prayer to bring blessings. It means, "In the name of God, the Infinitely Compassionate, the Infinitely Merciful."
5. This phrase means, "I seek forgiveness of God."

like a pulsating light that appeared to be glowing in rhythm with our chant. I could feel my heart's longing lifting me to an unfamiliar state. I wanted to melt into this living wave of light. I wanted to open my arms and let it carry me away. The crescendo of the "*Allah*" chant was followed by a chant of "*Hu*."[6] The resonance of our voices went to an even higher level, and I felt like I was disappearing in the waves of sound. I could no longer hear my own voice, all of our voices became a single, unified voice that seemed to take us into an inner heart embrace where the energy of the previous chants is held in an unending whirling wave of sacred sound within our hearts. After the last "*Hu*," Selim Baba ended the *zhikr* with a beautiful recitation from the Qur'an.

At the end of the *zhikr* I felt a deep stillness. A peacefulness engulfed my heart. I felt whole and joyful in a way that I'd never felt before. There was more yet! Small booklets were handed out containing lyrics of songs. Kabir started playing a stringed instrument that I'd never seen before—later I learned it was a *saz*, a traditional Anatolian instrument used to play folk music. Kabir's wife, Camille, and two or three other friends beat large hand drums. We sang beautiful songs, that I later learned were called *ilahis*, about Divine Love, burning, whirling, humanness, longing, seeking, and courage.

Every day of the retreat we repeated this amazing cycle of meditation, spiritual conversation, *zhikr*, and singing. We also cleaned together, cooked together, ate together, and spent time coming to know one another. My heart felt full, overflowing with love, joy, and tenderness. And there was more yet to come. On our last evening together, Kabir shared with us intimate prayers of Prophet Muhammad in which he expressed his inmost feeling, his longing, his needs, his hopes and fears to his Lord. Kabir wanted us to learn to express what is in our inmost hearts in the same way. He wanted us to overcome our self-consciousness and inhibitions and pour our hearts out in the circle. He said we would keep going around the circle until no one had anything left to say.

A candle was lit and placed in the middle of the circle and the lights were dimmed. We sat quietly for a few moments waiting for the first brave soul to speak. It was awkward in the beginning

---

6. This is literally the third person pronoun "He" in Arabic. It is used by Sufis to invoke the unknowable Divine Essence.

Introduction

but then something opened up and each person started to express themselves with beautiful, unrestrained intimacy that quickly brought out sobs by many in the circle. We kept going around and around and the tears kept flowing as our hearts opened and were held in loving tenderness by everyone in the circle. I was sobbing uncontrollably as all of my inhibitions left me. I cried as I called out from the depths of my heart to my Lord. I cried as I felt the rawness of emotions of each person calling out in longing and love. I don't know how I was able to withstand this avalanche of emotions flowing out of me and flooding into me. I thought my heart was going to burst. Then the wave started to subside and gradually stillness filled the circle as our hearts were emptied and our bodies reached a state of peaceful surrender. The lights were turned up again and there were embraces and soft laughter and a feeling of joy all around. Then I heard Selim Baba who was seated at the opposite side of the circle call out to me, "Hey Mahmoud! How do you like love Sufi style?"

Love, Sufi style. This is what I tasted on Mount Burke (we would later come to call it Mount Barakah[7]). I was drunk with love, my heart was cleansed and softened by the tears. A deep understanding was received that I could not have attained on my own or in any other way that I knew of. Kabir and Selim Baba were saying to me what I knew to be truth within my inner being but could not find words to express myself. A fire of longing was ignited in my heart that felt irresistible. I felt something surging within me, like some ancient deep sound, calling me to return.

Yes, this was Love Sufi style. As I came to know the community of lovers in our Sufi circle it dawned on me that I was witnessing the remaking of the first community of Muslims around the Prophet, and in America no less! It felt like I was taken to the early days of Medina among the small group of devoted companions of Prophet Muhammad. The sincerity, devotion, commitment, service, compassion, acceptance, truthfulness, and unconditional love amongst us reminded me of those intimate companions of the Prophet, those who understood and carried the teaching in their hearts. Those early companions of the Prophet were with him because of love. They loved him and in loving him they loved God. I felt so grateful to have been brought

---

7. This word means "blessing."

into this circle and humbled by the beautiful hearts who were there.

The Sufi School

The Sufi journey is a journey in Love, by Love, to Love. All genuine Sufi paths lead to the same Reality, that is to the realization of the Divine Love that is at the core of our being. We come to know this Divine Love through the integration of our scattered self into a unified, holistic human being. Once we come to know that we are this Divine Love (*Rahmah*[8]), we can then manifest it into the world. This is the meaning of being a *khalifah*[9] of Allah on earth. When we are capable of manifesting Divine Love, we realize our full humanness, we become Children of Adam.

A Sufi school is a school of Love devoted to the realization of the full humanness of its followers by transforming their hearts and perfecting their character. A Sufi school is a moving caravan that transports the hearts of its students on their journey, hence Sufi schools are known as "Paths." The Sufi journey is the spiritual foundry that forges mature human beings. The Sufi journey is not a solitary one, it is a journey of sincere companionship, devoted friendship, and selfless service. The ultimate purpose of Sufism is to carry on the sacred trust stated by Prophet Muhammad, "I have been sent only to complete nobility of character."[10]

The Sufi school's foundation is built upon the relationship of unconditional love between the Divine and the human being. It is remarkable that the Sufi way to non-duality is to realize the relationship of profound love between the human heart and the Divine, which is the essence of our being. It is through this seemingly dualistic relationship that the human heart can be purified from the accretion of learned habits, false beliefs, social

---

8. This word is commonly translated as "mercy" or "compassion." It holds deeper meanings. Its root is "womb" and so it holds the meaning of that unconditional love and protective embrace that holds us, nourishes us, provides for us, and ultimately births us.
9. This word means "successor" or "vicegerent" and in the Qur'an is used to refer to the purpose of human existence in the world.
10. "*Innama Bu'ith-tu Li'utammima Makaarimal Akhlaaq.*"

conditioning, and the false identity of the ego. The Sufi path can bring the human being to a state of unity with our essential self,[11] which in Islamic terms is to reach *tawheed*.[12] When we are in *tawheed*, we have returned to our Lord.

Each particular Sufi school is founded upon the oral transmission of prophetic wisdom through a living saint, a friend of Allah. The saint, or friend, is usually referred to as the *shaikh* or *pir*.[13] Every *shaikh* transmits to his or her disciples the teachings that they themselves received from their *shaikh* in a human chain of great souls that reaches all the way back to Prophet Muhammad. Usually, the school is established by the immediate followers of the saint after the saint passes on. A *shaikh* may or may not designate a successor to continue the chain of transmission. Although all Sufi schools ultimately have the same purpose, each has a particular form and practice that is suitable to the temperament of its followers.

The Mevlevi School

The Mevlevi Sufi path is named after the great saint Mawlana[14] Muhammad Jalaluddin Rumi (Mevlana in Turkish) and was founded by his son Sultan Veled, who established its particular method of teaching and forms of practice eight centuries ago. All genuine Mevlevi communities follow the general methods and practices established since the time of Sultan Veled.

The Threshold Society is a continuation of the Mevlevi *tariqa* and is part of the International Mevlana Foundation, headquartered in Konya, Turkey. Its *shaikh*, Kabir Helminski, was given the permission to teach (*ijazah*) by the late Celalettin Çelebi Efendi, 21st generation direct descendent of Mevlana Rumi, who was then the head of the Tradition.

The Threshold Society has been working for decades to develop an authentic expression of Sufism that is relevant to our time, civilization, and culture and at the same time holding true to the tenets of the spiritual guidance transmitted by the Prophet

---

11. The essential self is that which remains after our ego has melted in the fire of love.
12. This word literally means "to make one."
13. Both shaikh and pir hold the meaning of "elder," or "wise sage."
14. Mawlana means "our master, friend, protector."

Muhammad and followed by Mevlana Jalaluddin Rumi.

The work of the Threshold Society begins and ends with presence. Presence is essential to the spiritual awakening of the human being. Presence can best be understood as the inner capacity to consciously witness the context as well as the content of our experience. The development of this capacity transforms our attention, our will, our identity, and the quality of our emotions. In short, presence changes the meaning of our lives.

The Threshold Society focuses on the development of its students' capacity for conscious breath, conscious movement, conscious sound, conscious listening, conscious attention, conscious self-expression, and conscious service. The practices and activities of the school are carefully designed to enable this development. The Mevlevi circle, Mevlevi *zhikr*, Mevlevi *sema* (the whirling dervish ceremony), Mevlevi music, Mevlevi kitchen, and Mevlevi *sohbet* are all designed to develop these capacities within the students. The development of these capacities culminates in expressions of exquisite beauty. Throughout the past 800 years, Mevlevi dervishes have produced beautiful music, poetry, songs, and ceremonies.

What holds and integrates these practices and methods is an important capacity known as *adab*, or spiritual comportment. *Adab* can best be understood by reflecting upon a tradition of Prophet Muhammad. One time, as the Prophet and his companions sat in their circle, his cousin Ali asked him, "O Messenger of God, you and we grew up in the same community, and learned the same language. Yet you express yourself in ways that none of us have known before. How is it so?" The Prophet replied, "*Addabani Rabbi fa ahsana ta'dibi.*"[15] Which can be translated as, "My Lord bestowed an *adab* upon me that is most beautiful." From this tradition we can understand *adab* to mean the human capacity for self-expression and the highest form of *adab* is the expression of beauty. In the Mevlevi school, *adab* is the capacity to express oneself in the most beautiful way, at the right time, in the right place, with the right people.

---

15. This tradition can be found in Suyuti's *Al Jaami' Asagheer*, in Saraqusti's *Al Dalaa'il*, and Abu Na'eem Al Isfhani in *Tareekh Isfahan* among other sources.

Introduction

The Circle, Zhikr, and Sohbet

The Sufi circle is the container that holds the hearts of the dervishes and serves as the ground of connectedness for the spiritual community. The circle is itself a form of practice. It is a conscious container receiving the energy of Divine Love and transmitting the teaching to the community. The way the circle is formed, the way in which the dervishes sit and hold each other within it, the way the dervishes consciously connect their hearts and breaths to each other within the circle during *zhikr*, the way attention is consciously directed and held upon the *shaikh* as he holds *sohbet*, the way that words are spoken and shared, all come together to form a crucible in which the hearts of the dervishes can melt in the fire of Divine Love. Often, when one is in a state of presence, the vibration of Love flowing within the circle can be felt in the heart.

Zhikr is the heart of Sufi practice. *Zhikr* literally means to remember. What are we remembering? In one of the deeply mystical verses of the Qur'an, the Divine Voice speaks of a pre-eternal covenant between every human being and their Lord, Sustainer, Educator, and Nourisher (*Rabb*).[16] In this covenant, all of us bear witness that Allah is our *Rabb*. What is remarkable and deeply mystical about this covenant is that it happens *before* any of us come into physical existence. We witness while we are only a possibility in the reproductive organs of our parents. This moment of witnessing is known in Sufi teachings as the "Covenant of *Alast*." The word *Alast* comes from the question in Arabic, "*Alastu birabbikum?*" ("Am I not your Lord?")[17] to which we all answer, "Yes!" *Zhikr* is the process that awakens our hearts to remembering that we said "Yes" to our *Rabb*, that is, that we know at the core of our being that we have a *Rabb*.

In the Qur'an, the Divine Voice declares, *Remember Me, I remember you!*[18] From this we can understand that *zhikr* is a mutual, intimate discourse between the human being and the Divine. This reciprocity becomes evident in one's heart when at times we

---

16. Among the meanings of *Rabb* is "that one who holds and cares for us until we reach completion."
17. Qur'an 7:172: *When your Sustainer took the progeny of the children of Adam from their loins and caused them to witness of themselves, "Am I not your Sustainer?" They said, "Yes, we witness."*
18. Qur'an 2:152: *Fazhkuruni Azhkurkum.*

realize that we are being called to what brings us to wholeness, that we are being guided to what will heal us, that we are being shown what we need to see, to stand in Truth.

This remembering is made possible by a process of repeating the name of our *Rabb* (usually Allah, but it can be any of the Divine Names)[19] silently and out loud, alone and in community. This calling out of the Divine Name purifies our hearts and allows the Divine Light to emanate through every particle of our being, awakening our consciousness to a profound truth: that we exist because of Love in a universe of limitless Love. We come to know that Love is the cause of everything.

Zhikr is a subtle secret in the inmost heart of the human being. *Zhikr* is like a fire that kindles a love in our hearts like no other love we could possibly know. In time, with regular repetition, the energy of the *zhikr* becomes intrinsic to our being. The vibration of the Divine Name is felt with every breath that we take, and we experience a deeply intimate relationship within ourselves with our essential self, that is with our *Rabb*. This relationship serves to guide us, to strengthen us, to manifest through us Divine Qualities such as Love, Gratitude, Patience, Forgiveness, Generosity, Nobility, and much more. Through this intimate relationship with our essential self we become more and more integrated, more in Oneness; gradually our hearts are healed and the experience and meaning of our lives is transformed.

The *sohbet* is the main method by which the wisdom of the Tradition is transmitted by the *shaikh* to the students. Because Sufism is an oral tradition that is transmitted from heart to heart, the *sohbet* serves as the medium by which the wisdom of the Tradition is called upon and shared with the dervishes.

The *sohbet* usually starts with a recital or reference to a wisdom from the primary sources of the Tradition. These primary sources are the Qur'an, the traditions of Prophet Muhammad, the *Mathnawi* and *Divan-i-Kabir* of Mevlana Rumi, as well as the texts of some of the great Sufis such as Imam Ali, Ibn Arabi, Shamsuddin Tabrizi, Hallaj, Ibn Ata'llah, Ibn Abbad of Ronda, and others. This is not just a reading from a text. In a Sufi circle, when the *shaikh* recalls a wisdom from the Qur'an, or from

---

19. Although the Divine Names are limitless, traditionally we work with 99 Names.

Introduction

the Prophet and great saints, his heart connects with the Unseen, and this in turn connects the circle through the *shaikh's* heart to the heart of Prophet Muhammad, and the ocean of Divine Love flows to everyone in the circle. This is what is known as *barakah*, which is the energy of love that is accessed and received by the circle.

The *shaikh* serves as the channel through which the love, blessing, and the teaching flows. The more the *shaikh's* heart is purified and clear, the more the light of the Prophet emanates through him. The *shaikh* takes on the character of the Prophet to the extent that his ego has melted in the fire of love. The *shaikh* whose ego has melted becomes a humble servant of the Prophet, transmitting the prophetic guidance to the dervishes in the circle. As the *shaikh's* heart expands in Love's ocean, his words become the living Qur'an, penetrating deeply into the hearts of the dervishes, giving each one exactly what they need at the moment. The *shaikh* whose ego has melted realizes the station lovingly and humbly expressed by Mevlana, "I am the servant of the Qur'an and the dust beneath the footsteps of the Prophet." The teaching from the *sohbet*, when it is received and held in the heart of the dervish, becomes guidance that helps in the purification of the heart and the taming of the ego.

This Work of Love

This book will take you, the reader, into the heart of the Threshold Mevlevi circle where you can experience some of the spiritual conversations that have been shared over the years by Shaikh Kabir Helminski with his dervishes.

As one of the dervishes who worked on editing this book shared, "This book allows one to step into a stream of teachings that are both ancient and modern, sometimes simple and elegant, other times very deep and essential for the transformation of the heart and soul."

As you sit with this book, you will come to know about the purification of the human heart, the taming of the ego, spiritual companionship, realization of will, Divine Unity and integration of self, courage, devotion, truthfulness, and melting in the ocean of Divine Love. You will get a taste of the beauty of this ancient wisdom, of its sublime forms of expression in the sacred text of the Qur'an, prophetic traditions, and the poetry and aphorisms of the great spiritual masters of Sufism.

You may just fall in love! These *sohbet*s contain within them the energy of love. Many of the dervishes who make up the Threshold Society community fell in love with the Tradition while listening to *sohbet*s. As one of the dervishes who transcribed many of these *sohbet*s shared, "With the transcribing of each *sohbet* there was a falling in love with the art of spiritual conversation. I fell in love deeply with this Path, with my teachers, and above all with my *Pir*."

For each dear soul who worked on bringing this book into the world, this has been an offering of love in devoted service to the Mevlevi tradition. This work started in 2009 and continued over the ensuing decade by dervishes in the USA and the UK who meticulously transcribed 118 *sohbet*s. This volume contains 30 *sohbet*s that have been edited up to this point under the guidance of Shaikh Kabir Helminski. Care was taken to ensure that Sufi terms, which are usually in Arabic or Farsi, were explained in English for the benefit of the readers who may not be familiar with these terms.

For the dedicated dervishes who gave their hearts, time, and effort to bring this book to fruition, it has been sacred work given freely for the sake of love. As one of the dervishes shared, "Capturing the spoken words with the ears of the heart and putting them into written words always felt sacred." Another wrote, "Listening to and writing down the words spoken by Kabir in his recorded talks, each time I felt transformed somehow, the words spoken as if right to my soul, softening and opening places in my spiritual heart, loosening knots in my thinking that I didn't even know existed, and, perhaps most precious of all, giving language and expression to deep currents of truth and wisdom that I immediately recognised, yet which my own thoughts and language could barely behold let alone express with such clarity and coherence. I am forever grateful for the profound love that I knew and felt transmitted straight to my heart with every word."

What Do We Need a Spiritual Path For?

I WAS TALKING TO SOMEBODY RECENTLY who, with a good heart, said, "I have no need for religion. I know what is right and what is wrong." I didn't comment or argue, but, actually, this brings up some very important subjects.

Do we need God? Do we need God to do and be good? The answer is no, up to a certain point. You can do good without God. You can be kind, generous, respectful, and sensitive to other human beings without bringing God into it. What's the significance of bringing God into it?

First of all, my sense is that people are led to various religions and mystical traditions by a yearning from within. Something in them feels unfulfilled. It's like an inner drive or hunger. It's not, "I want to follow a religion so I can be a good person." Or maybe it's more a sense of "I don't want to just be at home. I want to be together with others. I feel like I need to be in a holy place." There is something more than just being nice, kind, and all of that. There's a deeper yearning operating within humans who undertake a spiritual practice. There is something else calling us. These things are part of a bigger whole.

The second aspect is that what we mean by "religion" is a reality that calls to us from a higher level. It is aspirational and transformational. Throughout history we see that people have not been very good to each other. Something else has been needed. Muhammad said: "Verily, Allah when He created the creation, He personally prescribed for himself: 'My mercy prevails over My wrath.'" This gives us what we need. It provides a sense of something that is good. It is better than how we are. The soul longs for a state of perfection. It's an ideal that is also timeless and spaceless. It includes the ultimate freedom to just expand, to merge with all that is. It's a bit like meditation. We long for something that is ideally free, beautiful, good, and generous. This longing contrasts with our limited self. If we're honest and conscious, this self is not always quite like that.

We spend much of our time doing what we want to do, or doing what we have to do to attain some desires of the self in the short or long term. In other words, we are always at the center of our own choices, we follow our own desires, and there is little that we feel answerable to.

Most of the time, it's our ego, or *nafs*, that is pulling us by the forelock here and there. We see ourselves sent in more directions than we can possibly go. We ask the question, "Which of the many impulses of my own ego will I follow? I can't follow them all." That's the big struggle. The real question is: What is to be attained by following our own *nafs*? To say, "I have no need for religion," is to say that I'm satisfied following myself, above all. And what is attained by following a traditional teaching, especially one like Sufism that is grounded in a lineage of enlightened and morally exceptional human beings?

The spiritual path, the path of transformation, is about following something other than our own whims and desires, even when these are within a basic moral structure. With a practice like ours, you are able to break the unconscious momentum of your self's activities. You are able to come into the center of your being and be there, face-to-face, with the Divine. You learn to love that. There's always a continual relationship between these two elements: the limited, imperfect part of ourselves and the eternal, pure part. The self, in a way, is blessed by that unconditioned, pure being. It is nurtured and transformed by it because that part of ourselves is intimate with the Divine.

Spiritual practice can also be undertaken with ambition, in a self-serving way. It can be done with an unconscious ego sense of "I want to gain something for myself." That's not the best way to approach a spiritual practice, but no one's intentions are totally pure, free of self-interest. And ultimately the spiritual path is more in your self-interest than unconsciously following the demands of the ego. But the point is that we are practicing for the sake of something that gradually frees us from many forms of psychological tyranny—the tyranny of the ego, the tyranny of unconsciously needing to please others, of conforming to the worldly values around us.

There's a transformative power that exists in the nature of Reality. There is something that can almost miraculously transform human beings. We need that. It's *within* ourselves, yes, but not *as* our selves. It is not there as an object. This is a subtle, metaphysical distinction.

To invite God into a conversation is to open the door of mystery and possibility. It is not about an exchange between two people, with the thought of "I'll do this for you, maybe someday you'll do it for me." It has nothing to do with expectation. It's not a *quid pro quo*. It's something entirely of a different order and unpredictable.

And so on the spiritual path we choose to give a certain amount of time and effort to be in the company of the Divine consciously and intentionally. It's appropriate to have, as we have in our Tradition, times of the day dedicated to this. There are times when we make an effort to bring ourselves into the presence of God. In our Tradition there is a physical effort involved in worship—the postures of bowing and prostration during *salaat*, or the practice of turning.[20] There's a "doing," not just a "being" in Sufi spiritual practice. It's "doing" with "being." The physical efforts in the ritual prayer also are done in *time*. We undertake the ritual prayers at the times indicated, following what we believe to be a heavenly, ordained pattern, not merely at *our* convenience, not just when *we* want to.

Yet we're really quite free. We have much time to do what we want to do. We also have some time we must reserve for our relationship with the Divine. How much is "a little bit of time"? Is it five minutes or an hour? These are small periods of time compared to the 24 hours that are in a day.

---

20. A specific Mevlevi practice, also known as whirling.

Someone says,
"I must provide for my family.
I have to work so hard to earn a living."
He can do without God,
but not without food;
he can do without Religion,
but not without idols.
Where is one who'll say,
"If I eat a piece of bread
without awareness of God,
I will choke."

[Rumi, *Masnavi* II, 3071–79]

We fool ourselves by saying we don't have time for spiritual practice. How else will we take care of ourselves, our hearts, our souls?

There is a story in Rumi's *Masnavi*[21] about the relativity of our sense of time and the urgency needed to spur us on in this work:

Once there was a man who planted a thorn bush in the middle of the lane outside his home. Those who passed along that way complained to him about the inconvenience it caused, but he did nothing about it. All the while the thorn bush was growing bigger; the people's feet were bleeding from its pricks. People's clothes were torn by the thorns, and the poor passers-by were getting nasty scratches.

"Root it up!" the governor told him.

"Very well, one day I will root it up," the man replied.

So for a long while he promised "tomorrow" and "tomorrow"; meanwhile his thorn bush grew strong and thrived.

"Stop procrastinating," said the governor to him one day, "and finish the job. Remove this hazard."

"There is still plenty of time, uncle," the man answered.

"No, hurry up at once," cried the governor. "Stop postponing the work."

---

21. Rumi's six volume work of didactic poetry, also written as *Mathnawi*.

What Do We Need a Spiritual Path For?

Commenting on the story, Rumi says: "Blessed is he who profits from the days of youth to settle debts, in the days when there is still the power, the health, and strength of heart and vigor; before the days of old age arrive, when the roots of bad habits are firmly established, and the power to pull them up is diminished."

Don't put it off, don't wait too long. When we truly commit ourselves to a spiritual path and practice, something in Reality rises up to support us. The destiny of what we're designed to be becomes real, and the fate of unconscious behaviours is avoided. Or, even if not avoided, our mistakes become learning experiences, blessed by some invisible Mercy. As Yunus Emre said, "Ever since the glance of the mature fell upon me, nothing has been a misfortune."

***

So how do we begin to fulfill our destiny as spiritual beings? How do we enter into a real, experiential relationship with the Divine? We can reserve a portion of everyday life to strengthen our practice. In the ordinary places where our lives are lived, we can make an offering of time and space to be in the presence of God. Sometimes the offering may take the form of simple stillness. We stop what we're doing, disengage from our worldly preoccupations, and make ourselves still and quiet in every aspect of our being.

Sometimes when we're in nature, on retreat, or on a journey with friends to sacred places, we have the experience of feeling closer to the Divine. We feel that we slip into and remain much more easily in states of stillness, silence, remembrance, and awe. We can experience a practice more deeply. These experiences in holy places such as Mecca, Medina, Konya, Istanbul, or Jerusalem can provide a taste and fragrance of sanctity as we undertake our spiritual practices there. The everyday practices of our Path, however, help us to internally create that sense of sacredness independent of circumstances.

In our Tradition, we use the body to experience the presence of God. We can teach the body what it feels like to surrender to the Divine as our forehead touches the ground during our prayer. This is something the body needs to tangibly experience.

Remembrance in its most elementary, tangible form is to chant the names of God. Remembrance is everything. Our destination as spiritually developing human beings is to live our lives in such a way that we are completely within that continual remembrance. That is the world and universe we live in. It surrounds and informs us. It illuminates our perception and softens our hearts. It should also bring us joy and happiness. That is our reality, because looking at life through the distorting eyes of the ego is, at best, a secondhand reality.

The word for "remembrance" in Arabic literally means "to mention," yet we translate it as "remembrance." When you mention someone, in a way, you're remembering the one you are calling to mind. We are remembering our Origin, remembering that we come from God and to God we will return. People sometimes talk about how children have an open channel to the Divine because they just came from God relatively recently. Remembering our Origin is a fundamental truth that we need to call to mind. This is expressed in the *hadith* "Whoever belongs to God, God will belong to him or her."

In that sense, if remembrance is deep enough, complete enough, it is the Divine remembering in you. In the state of belonging to God, what you want is not different than what the Divine wants. And "God" wants what you want; there is then no separate "you" wanting. There is no duality or personal will pulling in the opposite direction.

Rumi calls that being under the "compulsion of love." He says to be utterly compelled by love every moment is the only freedom. Otherwise you're just digging your heels in. Sometimes, your very self is mostly resistance. Otherwise we would just know, do, give, and love. There would be no "ifs" or "buts," no hesitations and doubts. This is a journey and a process.

Nothing to Fear

THERE ARE A LOT OF DISTINCTIONS we could make about what fear is or is not. When we speak about fear it is possible to observe that there is a positive fear and a negative fear. The positive fear need not be called fear at all. We can give it other names like care, vigilance, or responsibility. When a mother tends to her child and has absolute concern for the child's wellbeing it is not fear. Likewise, in spirituality, it is possible to speak of having *taqwa*, a positive fear of God. Muhammad Asad translates *taqwa* as having God-consciousness. This is different than the word for fear. *Taqwa* is a vigilance and awareness of the effects of our actions.

Mevlana[22] Rumi makes a wonderful observation: "Fear turns some people into cowards and others into heroes. Fear causes some to retreat and others to charge further into battle."

In encountering the inevitable fears within human life there are always those moments where we ask ourselves, "What do we do now?" As we were breathing *ar-Rahman*[23] during our earlier meditation, the realization came that there would be less fear if we can be in the overflowing, compassionate, positive force reflected by that Divine Name, the Most Compassionate.

There is a teaching in Sufism that defines emancipation as "freedom from the fear of loss." It is also the definition of a dervish who stands at the threshold between slavery and freedom. Emancipation is a *maqam*, a spiritual station.

If fear is holding us back then we can make this our aim. Anyone who is going to be a dervish cannot afford to be timid. Timidity is not part of this Path.

---

22. In the Tradition, Rumi is usually referred to as Mevlana (Mawlana), which means "our Master."
23. The Infinitely Compassionate.

Mevlana says, "Be at home amidst dangers." He also says, "I've tried sanity and now I'll make myself mad." In short, he is recommending doing the opposite of what the ego wants. If our possibility is indeed to live "life abundantly" as Jesus proposed, then we can confront what in reality are minor fears that keep us isolated. This is part of making and choosing our own work.

There are some fears of loss so trivial that we need not allow ourselves to fall into them. As for the big losses, which we will all also experience, they present the opportunity for real faith, real strength, and real courage.

One of our teachers in the early days of our Path said that one of the things not allowed of the dervish is fear. We cannot afford to be defeated by our fears. We may experience some really rough times so that we can come to know this. The rough times are a gift too. Everything can become a good. Sin can lead to virtue and fear can lead to something beyond fear. The truth is that everything ultimately is a mercy.

Sometimes, fear occurs when we get into our heads. We usually start getting confused about all the choices put in front of us. We are taken over by thinking about all the things that may happen the following week or maybe even two years from now. We may find ourselves thinking about what the state of the economy might be, our health, and whether we'll still be respected.

In my own experience I am functioning better when I am living more through my intuition, making choices through an inner knowing. This deeper knowledge can be primed by asking a question like: "How would the Prophet Muhammad tackle something really big? Or his beloved companion Ali? Or his dear wife Aisha?" We can look at ourselves objectively and ask how we would do the same tasks. "How am I getting there? Maybe there is another way to move forward."

We all have our lives, our responsibilities, our jobs, and our challenges in a world that does not necessarily understand the spiritual dimension of life. How wonderful it is to have the spiritual connection to return to. We can return to that trust and connectedness. Something in us knows this. We can venture out into a world where we are in relationship, taking on responsibilities, and dealing with problems and fears, but remain aware there is something beyond time and space that is timeless, indestructible, and unconditioned. It may sound abstract but it is not a mental proposition. It is a Reality that we come to trust more and more. We come to trust it so much that if we were to die in the next minute we would say, "OK. What's next?" or "OK, I die and then what?"

Living in spirit means not being dependent on things turning out "all right." In the unconditioned and true perspective of Reality, everything already is all right. Maybe sometimes it takes a descent into suffering to know that we can handle things and get through them. Our faith and practice will have prepared us for that. In that moment, we know our practice and know what is. Whatever any moment may bring, there is that unconditioned Reality, the Infinitely Compassionate, *ar-Rahman*, the Infinitely Merciful, the *ar-Raheem*. There are people who have been tortured who know that. There are also people who have every reason to be in utter gratitude who do not know that. There are people who have everything a human being could possibly need or want and don't know that.

Our freedom and lack of fear will be measured by what we give through humble acts of service, generosity, patience, kindness, and self-sacrifice.

Our first *murshid*,[24] Suleyman Dede, never claimed to do anything himself. When Suleyman Dede visited the United States, he said, "God brought me to this country, and He has taken me to all these different places, and He has arranged for these meetings to occur, for people to come, and He has made me say certain things. It is really amazing because I am not doing anything."

There was a man who used to visit Suleyman Dede. One day the man informed Suleyman Dede that he was dying of cancer

---

24. A mature spiritual guide.

and only had a few months to live. Dede said to him, "Oh, brother, don't worry about that. Next week I'm going to the Aegean. I'll take your cancer and throw it into the sea. *Eyvallah!*"[25] Six months later, the same man showed up at Dede's house saying, "Thank you! Thank you! My cancer is gone." Suleyman Dede's only comment was, "Silly man. He thinks I could do such a thing as take away his cancer."

That's a hint of the dervish spirit. There really is no fear in dervishes. Every human being, of course, has concerns and anyone can be disturbed. But we never saw fear in Dede.

---

25. Literally, "Yes, God!" or I accept whatever comes from God as good.

Initiation into the Inner Life

IN CERTAIN ANCIENT CIVILIZATIONS and indigenous cultures there was often a process of initiation that young people would go through before they became adults. In some Native American traditions, for example, the initiate would be put out into the wilderness without any food or any other provisions for survival. He would have to rely on the Universe and his own soul. During the experience, the initiate would fast. He would experience himself confronting the Universe alone. He would be out there for a number of days. This would open up the initiate to a direct experience of something beyond the usual egoic mind and all of its concerns. The initiate would be thrust into an experience that would take him beyond his small, limited self.

Such a process existed in our own Tradition going back to the Prophet Muhammad, peace be upon him. What was Muhammad doing in a cave when the first revelations of the Qur'an began if not going through what Native Americans would call a "vision quest?" He received direct revelation and inspiration through this practice.

Many religions have forfeited an initiatory process and instead have settled for indoctrination. Virtually all religions that lack this initiatory process set about to tell people what to believe and what to do. They think that indoctrination is enough.

Ramadan is an initiatory process for us. It's one of the extraordinary things about our Tradition. Ramadan is just a little bit of fasting for 30 days, or however many days one manages with it. But Ramadan is also a shared experience and resonance with qualities of coherence. It's initiatory because you are in a direct experience of a different state of consciousness. It doesn't matter much what you believe about Ramadan. The different states of consciousness and coherence result from simply lightening up on food and drink.

Some of you who have been through the Ramadan fast know what we're talking about. It's really one of the blessings of this Tradition that is offered to us every year. We have the experience of joining invisibly with millions of others around the world. In a sense, we are vibrating in this greater field of resonance.

In our own Mevlevi tradition we also had a specific process of initiation, though we no longer practice it in its traditional form. The Mevlevi traditional initiation or education was called the *chille*, which was an extended period of training. Most people who undertook a *chille* were young. They entered the Sufi *dergah*, spent 1,001 days there in service, worship, contemplation, and developing talents through the arts, gardening, cooking, or crafts. The arts included music, poetry, and calligraphy.

The *chille* was a comprehensive education, but its goal was not just to transmit and receive information. It was an initiation. Every moment of one's day was occupied in Divine remembrance. This was a kind of active contemplation. Mevlevi Sufis did not spend long hours in meditation the way Buddhists do for instance. But that doesn't mean they were any less committed to developing those qualities of attention and presence that are developed in meditation.

Our meditation is very active. It's that deep meditative state carried into all aspects of life that makes for a very integrated type of spirituality. We still practice the process. Although we don't work within a 1,001-day time frame any longer, we can teach those same things at the same time as we are involved in everyday life. It could be described as a kind of apprenticeship.

There's a story about the great Sufi master Khair-e-Nassaj. On his way to Mecca he arrived at the gates of Kufa clad in a patchwork robe. There a man approached him and asked if he was a slave.

"Yes," he replied.

"Have you run away from your master?"

"Yes," he replied.

"I will take charge of you until I can restore you to your master," the man said.

"That is what I am seeking myself," said Khair. "All my life I have been longing to find someone who will restore me to my Master."

The man took him home and taught Khair the craft of weaving. For years he worked for the man. Whenever he called out, "Khair!" he would reply "Here I am!" At last the man repented, having seen his sincerity, perfect behavior, and intuitive powers, and having witnessed the constancy of his devotions.

"I made a mistake," he announced. "You are not my slave. Go wherever you wish."

This process is about creating or attaining coherence within the individual self. What do we mean by "coherence"? We know very well what it's like to not be coherent. We don't know which way to turn. We don't know what to do. How to choose this or that. And even when we do, we're still beset with second thoughts and distractions. At the beginning of the story of Khair, he is clad in a patchwork robe: fragmented. But from his master he learns to weave, which is the art of integration.

Coherence comes from a deep center, which is the heart. Ultimately it's the heart of the human being connected to Infinite Spirit. When the self is connected to the heart, and the heart is connected to God, you have coherence. It's really that simple. The practice we call "the remembrance of God" is the channel to that coherence.

Honestly, I can say as of today, after practicing remembrance of God for 40 or more years, I'm still asking myself, "What is it? What is the quality of my own remembrance?" It's not just being present, though being present is a good start. It's an infinitely developable capacity of the heart to sense a spiritual reality that is beautiful, intelligent, generous, and longing to be in relationship with us. In fact, the real action, the real energy, comes from there, and not from us. It comes from the Divine to us, and we can only respond to it.

So for me, it's a never-ending question. What really is it to open up the heart to the Divine Reality? Neither Divine Reality nor your heart have limits. What a human being is capable of, what we can experience, what we can know directly through spiritual perception is infinite, and it can deepen continuously.

Love brings coherence when a person has a strong heart, a quality of unconditional love, and when the person themselves becomes a source of love rather than looking for objects of love. That's also evidence of having attained a deep coherence. Yet another way to talk about this, is that there's a channel between your heart and the Infinite. The Infinite is itself the power of unity and coherence. It has the power to come into your heart and so transform your heart. When your heart has been touched by even a little bit of this spiritual energy, the heart is transformed.

When the heart is transformed, your very self is transformed. I keep expressing it in the simplest terms as if it were easy. It's simple. It may not be easy. It's simple because all we really need to do is to be able to give our attention to the Source of Being and bask in the radiance of that energy from the moment we wake up in the morning to the moment we go to sleep and through the night as well. We will be transformed by that.

Very little of this can be accomplished alone. We've met maybe a handful of people in our whole lives who won the spiritual lottery. They had their ego-selves deconstructed by the Divine, and were put into a state of relative selflessness. In some cases, it was a difficult and trying experience, because they had to rebuild their functionality to even live in this world. I'm not sure anyone would really want that, given a choice.

I think it would be better and more reliable to undergo this process in the context and within the support of a tradition involving a group that takes you stage by stage, so you develop a certain emotional maturity, relationship skills, ethical awareness, and skillfulness in living life. If we can combine these qualities with that process of illumination we have the best of all worlds.

This way we have a self that is useful to others, but it's an illuminated self. Those who just get blown away by the Divine may experience a kind of enlightenment, but they are in some respects even disabled by it until they can be put back together. Usually it takes a very mature person on the Sufi path to help them recover.

Sufis take transformation gently, as a developmental process of simultaneously developing human maturity and what we'll call the enlightenment experience. We keep these things in balance. This is really an experience of energized higher consciousness. We work with a teaching that comprehends the stages of development of the human being and includes spiritual practices to facilitate the process. This quality of coherence is more accessible when a group of people come into that coherence together.

Any group that focuses itself generates this resonant field of coherence. We're all affected by it. Our communities are profoundly affected by it. Louisville will be affected by what happens in this room, without a doubt. The effect will be proportionately greater to what you would guess it would be if you add up the energy of a few individuals in this room. We're not that many, but that's not how it works.

There was a group of 7,000 Transcendental Meditation practitioners, who for one day meditated on world peace. That day, violence in the world dropped 70%. The number of acts of terrorism and violence around the world fell significantly with only 7,000 people meditating on peace.

Ramadan is a time of exceptional resonance because a substantial portion of humanity enters a relatively coherent state. This is a benefit to all humanity, just as the prayers that are done by our and other traditions benefit all of humanity to the extent those prayers are truly conscious, truly coherent, and connected with Divine Love. This Love brings coherence into our inner experience and into the field of consciousness. It can even be measured electromagnetically. All these things have physical properties, even though they're fundamentally spiritual.

Unite with the Living

IF WE REFLECT on what fills our hearts and minds, we would find a constant preoccupation with the details of living. These typically fall into several categories: what is needed to meet our responsibilities; what is required to do the work we have to do to make a living; and communicating and interacting with others.

There may even be a fourth category. This is the category of trivial things to which we give our time and attention. The feelings arising in this category may include regret and wishing that we didn't concern ourselves in such a way.

As spiritual wayfarers, our choice to make space for the Divine in our lives creates a fifth category: relationship with the Divine. We may find ourselves questioning how much space we've devoted to the Divine and whether that space is of the right purity. We may wonder if we are sustaining our spiritual practices sufficiently to raise our vibrations so we can be living at the level we know we could be.

Yet no matter how lofty or banal these categories of content may be, one thing encompasses them all: *Haqq*.[26] The great prophets, saints, and masters, and, of course, Mevlana Rumi, all call us to *Haqq*. Their teachings point to a reality with implications that may dawn on us with a shock. The following poem, "Unite With the Living," from Book I of Mevlana Rumi's *Masnavi* is an example of such a teaching.

> When the torrent reached the sea, it became the sea,
> when the seed reached the corn field,

---

26. The Truth, the Absolutely Real.

it became the crop of corn.
When the bread reached connection with the human,
it became living and full of knowledge.
When wax and firewood were devoted to the fire,
their dark essence became light.
When the dusty stone of antimony entered the eyes,
it turned into sight and became watchful.
Oh, happy is the man who was freed from himself
and united with the existence of the living!
Too bad for the living one
who kept company with the dead!
He also died, life sped away from him.
When you run for refuge to the Qur'an of God
you have mingled with the spirit of the prophets.
The Qur'an is the states of the prophets,
those fish of the holy sea of His Majesty.

[*Masnavi* I, 1531–38]

"Unite with the Living" already holds surface meaning as a metaphor. Underneath, however, we can glimpse even greater depths of the Reality Mevlana is teaching us about: Oneness and shared Reality allow us to move toward Truth and to cultivate it. Mevlana tells us that whatever we sow in nonexistence, we reap in existence. He describes our relationship with Unity through his references to movement and transformation. The metaphors of "surrendering" to the fire, "entering" the sea, and "becoming" the corn crop hint at the natural sequence of events that occurs as the soul draws nearer to God. Everything has a covenant with God. The bread doesn't become food until the human being becomes hungry enough to long for food. The whole poem is advice for us. Mevlana tells us in rapid succession, "Be a candle but burn! Be firewood, but burn! Be a torrent, but to go to the sea! Be bread, but get eaten!"

The poem also teaches that the Qur'an is the state of the prophets, which is a very important idea. In telling us to run for refuge to the Qur'an, we are being told our lives and our spirituality are not intellectual processes. That is the state of the prophets. In reading the Qur'an, we can pray for the spirit of it to come into us. We try not to read it with just the conceptual, thinking mind. By doing so, something arrives and enters our perception and awareness through the subtle faculties of the heart.

By looking deeply into Mevlana's stories and poems, we can see how he is living in Oneness. We see that he continually enters into that Reality. He shows us how the whole of physical existence is a reflection of that Reality, which is really a non-dimensional point. We learn that we have a relationship with nonexistence. Everything in existence here that has a beautiful surface meaning also has a much deeper meaning and essence there, in nonexistence. In our relationship to what is beyond space and time, we sow and we reap.

Mevlana takes us far beyond our everyday concerns by putting them into a perspective that's shockingly different. This is the perspective of trust and faith, where all questions are answered. We could even say this perspective is a kind of bliss. From this vantage point, we can see all the things that we're so prone to be distracted by, to worry over, to be fearful about, and try to strategize and plan for. From this higher perspective, we experience dimensionless Reality as a oneness of pure abundance, guidance, beneficence, and love.

This unity of Reality is not meant to be considered only during moments of a person's spiritual practice. That would make the idea subjective. Science has shown this is an objective truth. Through research and verifiable experiments, science has proven that existence is a oneness in which each of us are profoundly related to each other. Studies have shown, for example, that there is a connection among people who come together and have been connected for years in meditation. The same applies to those united by worship and *zhikr*.

Even our technological innovations are increasingly reflecting the metaphysical unity of Reality. For example, "the cloud" works as an enormous centralized memory space that people all over the world can access and interact through. Mystics know the metaphysical version of the cloud has always existed. The technological cloud reflects the metaphysical unity of Reality. Our souls are united in a non-dimensional point.

There are aspects of ourselves that provisionally seem discrete and separate. On one level, we relate to each other as separate beings with varying preferences, egos, thoughts, opinions, and points of view. However, in another dimension we're experiencing something simultaneously together. There has been evidence of this throughout the ages. One example is the simultaneous formulation of calculus in the seventeenth century by Isaac Newton in one part of the world and by Gottfried Leibniz in another. There are many other examples of events that are experienced and discoveries made by different people in different places at the same time. Even in the spiritual world, we learn, for example in *al-Futuhat al-Makkiyya* by Ibn Arabi—the Andalusian Sufi mystic, poet, and philosopher—about spiritual insights he received that were accompanied with knowledge that other people in other parts of the world were receiving the same insight at that same time.

Mevlana's poems say many of the same things. For example, in a well-known quatrain he tells us:

Out beyond ideas of faith or denial—*iman* or *kufr*[27]—
there is a field.
I'll meet you there.
When the soul lies down in that grass
even the words *you* and *I* have no meaning.

Another poem, "The Voices of the Holy" from Mevlana's *Masnavi*, teaches us about this all-encompassing Reality and its constancy:

Truly is there any fair thing
that has not one day lost its luster

---

27. Qur'anic terms which literally mean "faith" and "denial" (often mistranslated as "belief" and "unbelief").

Unite with the Living

or any roof that did not become a floor?
except the voices of the holy in our breasts,
that resound like the trumpet of resurrection?
By their hearts all hearts are intoxicated.
Through their nonexistence, we learn to truly be.
The saint is the amber that attracts our thought,
the delight of revelation, the inspired mystery.

[*Masnavi* I, 2078–81]

    The message of these poems is not an intellectual proposition. It is a matter of experience and perception. It is something to be grasped by the heart. The wisdom that's talked about is actualized through a completed human. That's when the sunbeam germinates the seed.

We Are the Context Not the Content

THE PROPHET MUHAMMAD, peace be upon him, said: "Pause and graze in the meadows of paradise when you pass them." Someone asked, "What are the meadows of paradise?" The Prophet answered, "The circles making remembrance of God. Go forth morning and evening in remembrance of God. But he who desires to know his standing with God should look at the rank he accords God. The rank God Most High grants to his servant corresponds to the rank his servant accords Him."

Here is a reminder that there is some kind of reciprocal relationship between your individual consciousness and that immense, infinite, compassionate power we call "Allah," or "God," or whatever other names.

There is also the beautiful reminder from the Prophet to seek out the meadows of paradise. The reminder is for people to remember God. The simplest way to remember God is to repeat the Divine Name with your heart. By doing so, you get into that vibration and shift your brainwaves into a different state. You orient your heart and soul to the Divine Presence simply through the name of God. Many traditions know and practice this, the Sufi tradition especially. And it's good to know the Prophet himself considered this so important, so essential.

Sahl ibn 'Abdallah observed, "Not a day passes but that the Exalted cries out, 'Oh my servant, you treat Me unjustly! I remember you, but you forget Me. I invite you to Myself, but you go to others. I take away afflictions from you, but you continue to afflict yourself. O progeny of Adam, what will you have to say on the day when you meet Me?'"

The Divine Grace is reaching out to us generously, yet we're somewhere else. We've got other business. We're forgetful. We are preoccupied with ourselves and our objectives. Although that's understandable, we still lose sight of the bigger picture. We lose sight of the way Reality is really organized. Divine Grace and Guidance are continually being bestowed on every human being. The agency is God. Blessings, guidance, inspiration are always available for every human being.

It is said that the Archangel Gabriel told the Messenger of God, "I've given your community something I've not given to any other community." The Messenger of God asked Gabriel, "What is that?" He replied, "It is God's words: *Remember me and I remember you.*"

It's interesting that this particular wisdom, this particular truth was given in the Qur'an. The Qur'an doesn't claim to have a monopoly on truth. This is one of the rare cases where Angel Gabriel is saying that there is one thing that has been given specifically and more explicitly in this revelation than ever before. It's not like this wasn't always the truth. But before the Qur'an, it had never been said and had never been presented to humanity so openly as this, *Remember Me, I remember you*.[28] It's an immediate relationship, an intimacy with the Divine.

It's often translated, "Remember Me, and I will remember you." But there's no future tense here, there's only the present tense. This is really, *Remember Me, I remember you*. What could that be about? What could be going on?

That moment in which you awaken to remembrance, is the Divine remembering through you? It's that close. Ultimate enlightenment may seem like it's for one in a million. But this remembrance and connection with the Divine is available right now to every human being. That illumination is very, very close. Take it. Right now. Welcome that state. Cultivate it. Make it a bigger part of your life. Make it more continuous. To develop that capacity in the human being is what we call development of being.

The Qur'an describes the Prophet Muhammad's ascent and entry into the presence of God. It says, *And his eye did not waver.*[29]

---

28. Surah al-Baqarah 2:152.
29. Surah an-Najm 53:17.

This means he had the capacity to give his full attention to that Infinite Presence. He even surpassed the Archangel Gabriel in being able to do that. Just think: a human could potentially get closer to that Divine Presence than an angel could.

Remembrance is the secret, unknown even to angels, intimately held between the human being and God. From the lowest to the highest, every level of humanity has its sin and its blessings. For the knower of God, forgetfulness of God is its own punishment, and remembrance is delight.

May we become so sensitive that a moment of heedlessness, a moment of forgetfulness, leads us to a moment of honest remorse.

Another way to put it is that we have a sense of loss with every moment that we spend in heedlessness. We can know that. We can live our lives in such a way and develop to a point where we're more sensitive to those moments when we are present with Divine Spirit. Then we do all that we have to do and whatever our life's work may be.

We have to work. We have responsibilities and obligations. However, all of that work can take place within this wider field of remembrance. Within this context we know we're in Love's universe. We're in the Divine Reality. We want to attend to details as responsibly as we can. Another saying of the Prophet is, "Live for the things of this world, your worldly affairs, as if you had all of eternity in front of you." In other words, don't live in haste. Give yourself the proper time. "But live also for spiritual matters as if you would die tomorrow." If each of us knew we were going to die tomorrow, these moments with each other would be precious. What would we say to each other? What would we talk about? Imagine what we would talk about if all of us together lived the wisdom of this *hadith*. We would be able to put everything in a new perspective.

The Sufi, the lover of God, is someone who lives in that perspective. For the Sufi, the eternal is present. The Sufi is aware of his or her death, not in a morbid way, but rather with incredible gratitude for life itself. Here we are! It's amazing!

Tradition says that it was revealed to the Prophet David, peace be upon him, "Rejoice in me and delight in my remembrance."

Mevlana Rumi, the inspiration of our Tradition, offers the following in a poem of his:

Expanding Friendship

Money and real estate occupy the body,
but all the heart wants is expanding friendship.

A rose-garden without a friend is indeed a prison;
a prison with a friend becomes a rose-garden.

If the pleasure of friendship did not exist,
there would be no reason for men or women to exist.

A thorn from the friend's garden is worth more
than a thousand cypresses and lilies.

Love sewed us securely together.
We owe nothing to the needle and thread.

If the house of the world is dark,
Love will find a way to create windows.

If the world is full of arrows and swords,
the Armorer of Love has fashioned our defense.

Love itself describes its own perfection.
Listen and be speechless.

[*Divani Shamsi Tabrizi*, 1926]

This kind of poetry grows in resonance over time. The more you read of it and of Rumi, the more bells go off in the heart and the more overtones you hear. There are some really important essential things expressed in this poem. Silence is not a lack of words. Silence is presence itself.

In a Sufi circle one of our primary objectives has to do with opening up our inner life. This develops a capacity of the soul to sustain a certain kind of consciousness.

That consciousness is not unlike what some call "mindfulness." We call it "presence." One dimension is becoming present to our own inner space and allowing the spaciousness to open up. That spaciousness is usually filled with a lot of content, thinking, emotion, desires, and distractions.

We tend to focus on the content. We think we are the content. An inner voice making statements like "I'm happy," "I'm sad," "I feel good about myself," "I feel terrible about myself," is the typical content of our inner space. But what each of us essentially is, is not the content, but rather the context. Our essence is a frame of consciousness. It is a capacity for seeing and perception. Beyond any kind of belief or religion, there is the reality of opening up inner and outer consciousness.

This process of mindfulness is more than a way to achieve stress reduction and relaxation as it has been and is being used in the corporate world, pop psychology, and academia. Mindfulness is just a first step.

We're intending to awaken a capacity to see and to be present. Ultimately that capacity is going to lead to something quite extraordinary, aside from ourselves, aside from who we think we are. Ultimately it's going to lead to a relationship with what we could call "Divine Guidance," "Wisdom," and "The Source of Cosmic Love" itself.

It's said in our Tradition that the human heart is a threshold between two worlds. The threshold is between the limited material world and the infinite spiritual reality. The heart is the threshold. We should be on that threshold all the time, bridging these two worlds.

When we live in that reality and are aware of that presence, we are in remembrance. It changes everything. We can realize that we are not just the content of our experience. We're also this beautiful context, which is divine and purposeful, guiding us stage by stage to deeper and deeper truth. Every stage of our life, if we're seekers, leads to a greater richness of meaning in our lives. Then we can be grateful even for the thorns because we know it has come from the Beloved.

All the heart wants is expanding friendship. It is not the kind of friendship that is a social satisfaction and can even lead to dependency and attachment. Rather, it is the friendship of other conscious hearts, who are in that state of remembrance and in that state of coherence and resonance. That's what lifts and heals us.

That's why Sufis have their *dergahs* and communities. Sufism is not arranged as an individual tutorial. It's not a path for hermits. There may be periods when one benefits from solitude. However, there's transformation in friendship. The transformation results from knowing one another and accepting the truth that everything is purposeful. Whoever walks through the door of the Sufi *dergah* has been invited. We're all friends of the Friend.

Community is part of the mechanism of transformation. Because Western society is so individualistic, we find ways of avoiding relationship and seek transformation that will occur at our own convenience or according to our own preferences. Sometimes people reach the stage where they say, "I might be better off alone. I think I'm getting enough of this spiritual stuff that I could do it myself." They give up the friction of relationship and the challenge of it, and retreat into their own world.

It's not usually a healthy sign. However, everyone is free. On this Path, no one is coerced. It's not a cult. There's no group pressure. If somebody walks away from a Sufi circle, nobody chases after them, except perhaps out of friendship. Sufis don't interfere with anybody's will. We all have free will. We are happy to find friends who share a common yearning. We are helped and healed by that yearning. We are healed by each other.

The Body is a Servant

MEVLANA SAYS, "O Body, you are wonder within wonder within wonder!" Spiritually developed people know the body as an instrument of consciousness. Some say we have bodies on different levels. There are metaphysical teachings regarding the astral and causal bodies. But what I want to focus on and affirm is something very practical.

On the one hand, we can be the kind of human beings who are tyrannized, ruled, and mastered by our own bodies. For example, if we have pain, it may totally preoccupy us. Emotions that are felt by the body can also rule and master us.

The Qur'an asks whether the one who has many masters is the same as the one who has one master. The practical side of this is that we're enslaved to a vast number of things if we allow ourselves to be mastered by our senses and this world. In this condition, we may be pursuing random desires, our attention flitting among distractions, fears, worries, and considerations of how we look and what people are thinking of us.

Our spiritual development is a development of mastery, pure and simple. The mastery is coming from a different level of being and reality. There is a capacity that can develop in a human being for "seeing," for being present, and for being able to be in relationship. The more we know that level of reality, the more our I-ness is centered there. With that centeredness there is greater possibility of mastery over our inner life, our bodies, our physical sensations, our own healing, and all sorts of other things. Spirituality is about awakening awareness at a certain level of reality that is conscious, intentional, loving, and positive.

The spiritual nature of the body arises from its being a transformer of subtle energies. This is a really big truth. Everyone's body can transform subtle and not so subtle energies from one kind of energy into another. Spiritual practice in all its many forms is a process of refining the energies that are available to us. In contrast, mindlessly giving in to satisfying the body dissipates energy. It lowers the vibrational rate of the cells in the body. Spiritualizing the body's desires by periodically fasting, exerting physical discipline, and bringing awareness into everything enhances the pleasure of the senses. Taste and fragrance are examples of senses we can spiritualize.

The spiritualization of desires frees us from slavery to the senses. A stanza from the *Masnavi* explains:

> The cause of narrowmindedness is multiplicity:
> the senses are drawn in many directions.
> Know that the world of unification lies beyond sense:
> if you want unity, move in that direction.

[*Masnavi* I, 3099]

This is a metaphysical proposition. We may be a little surprised to see multiplicity associated with narrow-mindedness. We think multiplicity goes out and covers everything, especially when the senses are drawn in many directions. Instead, Mevlana is telling us the world of unification lies beyond sense-perception.

"Beyond sense" means moving to another level, in the direction that can encompass sense-experience as well as metaphysical qualities of awareness. In that level, the soul can be a dancer. Rumi shows us this in his poem in the *Masnavi*, "Have You Lost Your Horse?":

> So long as the heart does not see
> the Giver of its conscience,
> so long as the arrow does not see the far-shooting Archer,
> one who is that blind thinks his horse is lost.
> He's stubbornly spurring his horse along the way,
> but he thinks his horse,
> sweeping him onward like the wind, is lost.

> That scatterbrain runs from door to door
> searching everywhere and asking everyone,
> "Who stole my horse; where is he?"
> What is that you're sitting on, O master?
> "Yes, this is the horse, but where is the horse?"
> O you in search of your horse, be aware of yourself!

[*Masnavi* I, 1114–19]

By saying, "Be aware of yourself," Rumi is telling us about the importance of experiential knowledge. We run around thinking we're missing something, and what we are looking for is right here.

The teachings of Sufism are built on inner experience, not a belief system or a philosophy. The inner experience includes different levels of reality and presence. The physical level—the world of bodies—is one world we're in. However, we're also in other worlds simultaneously. Each level of presence has a knowledge particular to it. To be present and conscious brings with it the knowledge of presence at that level. Other levels include the level of emotions, the level of thoughts, and the psychic level. Beyond these, there is the level of Divine Qualities, the level of the Divine Names.

In *zhikr*[30] and in certain other Sufi practices we work with the Divine Names. To some degree, we will have an experience of the Divine Qualities, the Beauty, Majesty, Subtlety, Life, and Light. Beyond that, there is moving towards levels of union with the Divine Source. Fundamental to this teaching is the possibility for a human being to integrate all of these levels while remaining grounded in physical presence. In other words, it is possible to not be limited or preoccupied with just the physical body, but rather to bring all those levels down to include our experience of being embodied. This could be very different from the less conscious experience of suffering with the body, catering to it, or just enjoying it in a physical sense.

---

30. The remembrance of God, also transliterated as *dhikr*.

Let me share some words of the Turkish Sufi Yunus Emre from the collection of his poems entitled *The Drop that Became the Sea*.

> We entered the house of realization,
> we witnessed the body.
> The whirling skies, the many-layered earth,
> the seventy-thousand veils,
> we found in the body.
> The night and the day, the planets,
> the words inscribed on the Holy Tablets,
> the hill that Moses climbed, the Temple,
> and Israfil's trumpet, we observed in the body.
> Torah, Psalms, Gospel, Qur'an—
> what these books have to say,
> we found in the body.
> Everybody says these words of Yunus
> are true. Truth is wherever you want it.
> We found it all within the body.

Yunus brought heaven to earth. He brought heaven into his body. He found heaven in his body. I trust that Yunus, who is one of the greatest mystical poets of all time, would not make this up. He would only talk about what he had experienced.

The Qur'an says, *We created the human being in the most beautiful proportions.*[31] It does not say "the body," but rather, *the human being*. This must include the body and much more.

Our aim is mastery over the body. Mastery stems from a conscious relationship with our bodies, our emotions, our thoughts, and the higher levels of being human. Progress towards mastery begins quite simply. We start by just being aware, breath by breath. We learn to be more intentional with our life. We learn to be more patient, less judgmental, and less reactive. To do those things requires a spiritual energy that has to be kindled and awakened.

---

31. *Surah at-Tin* 95:4.

How to be fair to the body is a skill we can and should learn as well as practice. This skill includes treating the body well enough so that it doesn't get in the way of our spiritual practices and become an obstacle. Sufis have used the practice of giving up sleep to go to another level. However, too little sleep might make us irritable. In this case, we practice discernment about the practice of limiting sleep. Giving up the things we usually do with or for our bodies can go both ways. Too much sleep, too much food, and too much talking can bring us down.

We'll continue to learn to observe our relationship with our bodies. We should love and respect our bodies as long as we're still alive. As we exist in such an engaged and deliberate relationship with our body, we will see, over time, the passing of obstacles.

We can train the body with love so that it becomes a faithful servant rather than a tyrant. Love plays a larger role as we go further into the realm of will, consciousness, intention, and inner mastery. Unity plays a role. These are attributes of that Higher Reality. We can't live in that Higher Reality without awakening those qualities. This next poem is from Rumi's *Quatrains*, called "The Reins of Love."

> I'm drunk from a cup engraved with the word "Love."
> The horse I ride has Love for its reins.
> This Love is a supreme work, but
> I am bound to the One who loves his slave.

[*Quatrains*, 256]

Mevlana's love is a conscious love. It is a love that includes a masterful awareness. This awareness is sustained by a quality that is conscious, aware, and coming from Love.

"The horse I ride has Love for its reins." In this case, the horse is the body. The body is a vehicle and provides a beautiful energy and capacity.

"I am bound to the One who loves his slave." This too describes a relationship. Mevlana is calling himself a slave. He is not saying he is an abject slave to some cruel, dominating power. He says, "I'm a slave to the One who loves me."

The fact that we're slaves to the One who loves us means we're not slaves to anything else. There is something in us that is potentially a "master" in relationship to the body and a "servant" in relationship to the Real. With maturity and spiritual development, the soul gains a freedom from the body and is no longer limited by it. Along the way, we must take care of the body to balance its energies. This is absolutely essential to our wellbeing.

Somebody once asked a shaikh, "How are you?" The shaikh responded, "Still dying!"

We know the body is a wonderful, extraordinary, creative instrument which will also one day decline. It's possible as it does decline that our souls will come shining forth in a way they never have.

The Prophet Muhammad said, "Die before you die." We are being told to know the after-death state now, while we are alive. The mystics say that just as the embryo fears being born from the womb into this world, we fear our next birth. We fear being born from the womb of this material existence. The embryo can't imagine there is anything better than the warmth, comfort, and easy life it experiences in the womb. When it uncomfortably emerges into the expanded world outside the womb, it finds beautiful colors, fragrances, sensory experiences, and relationships. As human beings, we may similarly fear emerging into the expansive world that is beyond the boundaries of our egoistic existence. It's a goal of this spiritual path to be living in two worlds at once. By doing so, we can bring heaven to earth.

Polishing the Heart

ONCE THERE WERE SOME Chinese and Greek artists who were put in a gallery with a curtain in between them. Each group of artists was to create a masterpiece by which they would be judged. The Chinese painted incredible pictures on the walls. Meanwhile, the Greeks worked secretly; nobody could see what they were doing. When the curtains were pulled away, it was revealed that the Greeks had polished their walls into mirrors. All the magnificence of what the Chinese had created was reflected in the mirror made by the Greeks.

This story provides a brilliant image to illustrate the nature of presence and consciousness. "Polishing the mirror of the heart" is a common phrase in our community. Yet the experience of a heart being relatively empty and clear is not necessarily a common one; it is not something to be taken for granted or assumed. In our Tradition, we come together at least once a week as well as practice alone to do that polishing. This might give us some experience of our own heart being relatively clear and empty. Mevlana Rumi says, "When the mirror of the heart is polished, then the images and meanings of the Unseen might reflect there."

The "unseen" does not refer to some kind of mysterious, supernatural messages and visions. It may just be qualities like peace, forgiveness, hope, contentment, and gratitude.

Continuous polishing is like opening a whole dimension of being that wasn't there before.

Mevlana has a poem for us on this topic. It is from the *Masnavi*:

> The reflection cast from good friends is needed
> until you become, without the aid of any

reflector,
a drawer of water from the sea.
Know that the reflection is at first just
imitation,
but when it continues to recur,
it turns into direct realization of truth.
Until it has become realization,
don't part from the friends who guide you—
don't break away from the shell
if the raindrop hasn't yet become a pearl.

[*Masnavi* II, 566–68]

All Sufis know the work in its entirety is about polishing the mirror of the heart. We don't really know when we come together whose heart may be pure or attuned to the Divine Reality. But if some of us are—or even just one of us—then that reflection may be shared among the hearts that are gathered together. It is better yet if the Divine Reality is being reflected among most or all of the hearts that are gathered. When we polish away all the attributes of the false self, the attributes of the Divine will reflect not only in us, but *from* us.

This is why we're always working on polishing. Separative impulses, negativities, resentments, and any other attributes of selfishness have to be polished away to make our inner space reflective.

Resentment is one of the common forms of rust that can form on a heart. If there is any, it's important that we do our best to let it go. Any kind of negativity that we bring here interpersonally has got to be polished and let go for the sake of the welfare of the whole. This is a basic teaching. If there's something that needs to be said outside the group to heal hearts, then let it be said, let it happen outside the group.

In some Sufi lineages, such as the Bektashi tradition, every time the group meets, the *baba* will ask three questions. First he will say, "Is there anyone in this circle who has been hurt by another and wishes to bring that before us? Is there any couple having problems that they would like to bring before this gathering?" And finally the third question is, "Is there anybody with any need at all that they would like to put before us?"

Ninety percent of the time nothing is brought up. People know these things should be taken care of before they arrive to a gathering of hearts intent on remembrance and worship. In the Bektashi tradition, the *baba* will say after such sharing, "If so, *eyvallah*, then let us enter into the beauty of remembrance together," and worship begins.

For us, worship is essentially communion with the Divine. A community with a common vibration that orients itself to the Divine will very naturally and very easily be lifted stage by stage. The Qur'an promises: *Those who strive in Our way, We will guide*.[32]

It's more proper to remember the Divine and worship together than to do so alone, because alone we can suffer the illusion that somehow the individual self is the ultimate unit of Reality. We need to remember there's something beyond that. There's the inter-penetration of souls, the inter-penetration of the human and the Divine, of the earth and the earthly, and the heavenly within all of this. So, the reason for our being in community is that doing so reflects Reality, the Truth, the *Haqq*, and elements of that Truth that are reflected in each of us.

The need is to be near to those who are polishing their hearts until that reflection becomes certainty in your own heart. When we say "certainty" we don't mean "close-minded certainty." We don't mean something that shuts us off from reflection. The certainty is based on our experience of the Divine, which is intrinsically an experience of openness, not closed-ness. Imagine a certainty that is all openness and not a clenching of the mind. One day, that reflection may originate in your soul and my soul.

Here are some passages from the *Masnavi* with this message:

Remember the adage: "Men are mines."
One mine may be worth a hundred thousand.

---

32. Surah al-'Ankabut 29:69.

One mine of lurking ruby and carnelian
has more value than countless mines of copper.
O Ahmad, here riches are of no use!
What is wanted is a heart full of love and pain and sighs.

[*Masnavi* I, 2077–79]

The allusion in this passage is to the time when the Prophet, peace be upon him, (here referred to by Ahmad, a variant of his name) was talking and negotiating with some important people of a certain tribe and a blind man came seeking his help. The Prophet frowned and brushed him off, saying, "I'm busy with these important people." Later a *surah* entitled "He Frowned" was revealed. In that *surah*, God reprimanded Muhammad for that moment of mild disrespect to a human being who sought his help and for his preferring the privileged and the powerful. That's where this idea of human beings as mines arises. You don't know: a seemingly worthless person, a modest, unassuming person may be a mine of rubies.

What is the true value of a human being? What will be cultivated in ourselves? What will we do to beautify our souls and make our souls what they're meant to be?

Mevlana informs us here that what is wanted is devotion. The most beautiful qualities in a human being are love and devotion. The pain of this love is not like other pains. It's not the pain of self-pity, saying "Oh, poor me." It's a pain of intensity.

Rumi tells us there's something quite precious in the human soul that has a passion for communion with the Friend. He says: "What is wanted is a heart full of love and pain and sighs."

Mevlana tells a story that illustrates this in a passage in the *Masnavi*. In that story, Moses comes across a shepherd who is praying, so he stops and listens. The shepherd says, "Oh God, I love you so much that if you were to come down here and be right in front of me now, I would comb your hair for you. I would even pick the lice out of your hair! Oh God, I love you so much!" On hearing this Moses loses his temper. He harshly judges the shepherd for thinking that God has hair, let alone lice in his hair. In a state of judgment and self-righteousness, Moses berates the shepherd. We are told the shepherd leaves the scene, but Moses remains. God then comes to Moses and takes him to task. Moses realizes he's made a big mistake in judging the shepherd and so he sets out in search of him. Moses catches up and without waiting for the shepherd to turn, Moses begins to apologize for his treatment. The shepherd faces Moses. Mevlana describes the shepherd as being radiant and in a state of *marifah*.[33] Moses continues to apologize profusely, but the shepherd stops him and says, "No, you were completely right. I understand now. As it is said, even the mistakes of lovers have benefits."

People often hear at mosques that they should strive to accumulate material, intellectual, and spiritual riches by fasting, holding night vigils, and offering supererogatory prayers to escape punishment and sin and to gain rewards. I want to hear an imam that will say, "Let's hear the sighs that you have for the love of Allah. Let me see the pain you have as a result of separation from Allah."

Rumi says the more aware you are, the more spiritual you are *and* the more you suffer. He, and Hafez, and so many others have said: "The Sufi has nothing to do with Hell or Paradise, but only with God."

> Your true substance is concealed in falsehood,
> like the taste of butter in milk.
> Your falsehood is this perishable body;
> your truth is that exalted spirit.
> For many years, this milk of the body,
> is visible and manifest, while the butter,
> which is the spirit,
> is perishing and ignored within it—
> until God sends a prophet, a chosen servant,
> a shaker of the milk in the churn,

---

33. Spiritual realization, gnosis.

who skillfully shakes it, so that you might know
your true self, which was hidden.

[*Masnavi* IV, 3030-34]

A truth can only be revealed by falsehood. There is a *hadith*: "Falsehood troubles the heart, truth brings joyous tranquility." Life is a mixture of joyful tranquility and the heart getting troubled by seeing the falsehood.

The fasting of Ramadan, the Mevlevi practice of turning, the practice of ablution, and the ritual prayers are examples of truths or wisdoms that "shook the buttermilk" of society and that "churned" people. Together and separately they lead to ongoing transformation. None of us are ever the same after the shaking and churning that starts with any of these truths, wisdoms, and practices. Their lingering and persistent effects on us are relentless and abiding.

A man came to the Prophet Muhammad, peace be upon him, and said, "Ever since I got involved with you and this Way, my life has been really difficult. I've faced incredible challenges, internally and externally." The Prophet's response was: "Do you think that this *deen*[34] will let go of you until it's brought you to your destination?"

This story shows there's beautiful help being provided from the Invisible, if we make a gesture towards it.

---

34. Religion in its totality, the system of Divine Grace and Guidance.

Make God Your Companion in Every State

> The porter runs to the heavy load and takes it from others,
> knowing burdens are the foundations of ease
> and bitter things the forerunners of pleasure.
> See the porters struggle over the load!
> It's the way of those who see the truth of things.
>
> [*Masnavi* II, 1834–36]

THE QUOTE ABOVE IS AT THE BEGINNING of a chapter in *Living Presence*, called "The Alchemy of Effort." There's a truth that when we're intentional and affirm something, very often the affirmation brings up a denying force. It's not until we really decide to intentionally do something that we see resistances come up. Whether developing ourselves artistically, intellectually, spiritually, emotionally, or physically, there's a struggle that will go on between affirmation and denial. Expect that resistance. Yet there is a blessing in the struggle, because that is where the alchemy lies. That's where the transformation lies. The transformation through struggle does not happen at the level of affirmation and resistance.

If you just glide through life, looking for the path of least resistance, things may appear to be easy. But it is actually the practices and disciplines of the spiritual path that are the easy way, though they may look challenging and seem to bring difficulty at first.

The Qur'an says: *In His causes you ought to strive.* The Arabic word *jihada* could be translated as "strive." The real *jihada*, the real spiritual striving, is reconciling the energy or force from which we gain a new relationship with the struggle between intention and resistance.

The "causes" refer to "Divine causes." In his translation, Yusuf Ali puts in the parentheses "with sincerity and discipline."

The Qur'an continues by saying:

> *He has chosen you and imposed*
> *no difficulties on you in religion.*
> *It is the way of your father Abraham.*
> *It is God who has named you*
> *as those who are surrendered,*
> *both before and in this Revelation.*
> *That the Messenger may be a witness for you,*
> *and you be witnesses for mankind.*
> *So establish regular worship and give regular charity,*
> *and hold fast to God.*
> *He is your protector,*
> *and He is the best protector and the best helper.*
>
> [*Surah al-Hajj* 22:78]

The Qur'an tells us in this passage, *and God has not burdened you with religion.* This is a beautiful statement about the Path. We see the Path as something very broad and universal. It is, as it is said in the Qur'an, "The way of Abraham." It's that primordial faith. Very simply, that means one thing: place your trust and attention in the Divine.

The Qur'an says, *God has chosen you.* This means He has chosen anyone who has a longing for this spiritual reality.

But the teachings tell us there is another essential dimension to this striving, the all-important dimension of presence. There are actually three parts to striving: affirmation/intention, resistance/disappointment, and presence. At first when affirmation meets resistance, the struggle may be frustrating and seem fruitless in some respects. Everything seems to be only a clash of opposites. But with the support of presence, intention can summon Grace. With the help of presence we can not only formulate an intention but also ask the Divine to support our intention.

Intention based only in my own limited will is incomplete. All my limited will can do is make an intention to realize there is some work to be done, whatever that work may be. For us there's the work of transformation, transformation of the self. Do we ask for it? Do we call on the Infinite for a little help? A little mercy? A little strength? A little discipline?

When our striving comes from that higher level, when intention is enfolded with presence, we may understand the truth of the above passage from the Qur'an, and in this line in particular, *It is God who has named you as those who are surrendered.* You are lifted above the immediate clash of opposites and brought into a more spiritual perspective, surrendered, aware of Divine Support and Grace, no matter what the outcome. You can be an example of this surrender, this striving, to live in the Divine Way, the Way that reflects the highest truths.

In the fourteenth century, Ibn Abbad of Ronda wrote some letters of spiritual guidance to his students. Sufis most often wrote metaphysical works or works interpreting other texts, especially the Qur'an. It's rare to discover letters like this that really deal with people's everyday issues. We read from one of these letters:

> Praise be to God for the breadth of His Grace.
>
> I received your letter describing your present spiritual states. You expressed yourself well. The gist of your message is that you find some of the states you are experiencing despicable and not at all to your liking and that you do not find them conducive to approaching your Lord. You wish that you could find your way to, and live in, certain new states, which you fancy and regard intellectually as desirable and of a positive value.
>
> My dear Brother, you are being too severe with yourself and are acting inappropriately. You have pointlessly and unprofitably wearied your mind by spending your time that way. Worse still, it is positively harmful for you to concern yourself with such matters for they keep you from seeing the intent of the saintly mystics and keep you distant from the Sustainer of the Universe.
>
> I do, nevertheless, find your situation understandable since it seems you share the lot of countless others before you and still to come who have had the same experience. You

subscribe to their opinion that they are self-sufficient and strong enough to do as they wish whether in action or in repose and that they can be entirely heedless of the First, the Designer, the Disposer, the Dispenser of Decrees. That opinion in turn leads them to the wrong questions and to spurious answers by which they are diverted unawares from the Straight Path.

He then describes how people fall into different categories:

> There are those who engage in the ritual prayer, fasting, pilgrimage, the lesser pilgrimage, dhikrs, charity, teaching, service, deeds of devotion, et cetera, et cetera. But without finding consolation in them and, as you have described in your own case, find themselves in difficult spiritual states similar to yours.
> Then there are those who are content with all their outer activity and never want to stop being busy. However, when through laziness or boredom, or something in between these two, their resolve weakens, then they experience confusion and turmoil and they believe they have been banished far from God's presence.
> Then there are those who give no thought to spiritual practices and could not care less about them. They imagine they can handle anything that comes their way. Still others carefully plan their lives as if they were in control, and when the time comes they see their own carelessness and procrastination. They do not measure up and do not fulfill their promises. They postpone their intentions until some more convenient time and so on indefinitely.
> Then there are some who do not engage in religious practices and works but who, upon hearing stories of their forefathers in the faith and their fidelity to the prophetic example and their pleasing deeds, believe themselves quite capable of such things should they just make their minds up to do them. Then they say, "I will get to it when I'm free from such and such other tasks, and when I'm in the proper spiritual state." As I have already suggested, they spend their whole lives procrastinating.

Some other people are convinced that their lives are in total disarray and that they are capable of nothing whatsoever. That may be quite true. That is, they may be so either in fact or metaphorically speaking or perhaps they only imagine that to be the case. When these people hear of their exemplary ancestors in the faith or see a person who possesses their qualities they say, "No one like me is capable of that or has either the desire or power to accomplish such things." So they let it go altogether and do not resolve to make any effort.

I have observed all these false attitudes in myself and have noticed them in others. I have seen how these excuses can conquer our hearts.

On the other hand, the Mystics and those who are spiritually advanced concern themselves with the inner work. They are free from such frivolous excuses. They strive for the perfect realization of the Divine Unity from the start, for they make a solemn intention and pray in humility to their Sustainer so their hearts are aware of Him all the time. *They endeavor to make Him their Companion in all their spiritual states insofar as they are able. When God discerns that attitude in them He is Merciful to them by causing them not to pay attention to their own weaknesses or strengths in whatever they undertake or leave aside. Instead, He is their safeguard and protection. He guarantees their welfare and sustenance for they are His Servants and are dedicated to serving Him.* God Most High has said, "Is God not sufficient for His Servant?" Again, The Most High has said, "Say; Behold my Protecting Friend is God, Who reveals The Book, Who Befriends the Righteous." And in the Sacred Tradition the Most High has said, "I am with My Servant whenever he or she thinks of Me."

The difficult becomes easy and the struggle bearable for these Servants. God makes their every moment precious and significant. He establishes them in ease and in a Great Kingdom and in Him alone they move and take rest. On Him alone they rely. To Him alone they raise all their thoughts and aspirations. That is why this community is pre-eminent among communities. In one of the Traditions, God Most High is said to have inspired Jesus, peace be upon him, saying, "I will send forth a community after you. If they love what befalls them, they will give praise and thanks for it. If they hate what befalls them, they will be mindful of the reward in the next life and bear it patiently, even though they possess no understanding and no knowledge." Jesus, peace be upon him, replied, "O Lord, how will that be if they are without understanding and knowledge?" God answered, "I will give them of My Understanding and My Knowledge."

Prophet Muhammad's community is therefore especially one of liberality and ease. The community does not even despise troublesome burdens because what they desire is so readily available. This facilitation of every situation is made possible only through the contemplative vision of which I have spoken. God has said, may He be Exalted and Glorified, "God has laid upon you no hardship in religion. Yours is the community of your Father Abraham, this revelation as well as from the past. He named you Muslims, those who surrender, and the faith of that community is none other than surrender and the acknowledgement of the Divine Unity." Our Prophet, may God bless him and give him peace, has said, "those who put God at the center was the faith community of Abraham, upon whom be peace." A certain mystic commented on the words of the Prophet, may God bless him and give him peace: "They will find it easy and not difficult." The saying means they are led to none other than God. Therefore, anyone who leads you to the world is way-laying you and anyone who directs you towards external actions only wears you out. But the person who leads you towards God has given you good advice. My point here is to let you know that these people are subject to fewer of the errors that I have mentioned. That is, errors relating to lack of genuine self-knowledge, an inaccurate assessment of their ability and their own strength. If this was not so, they would possess neither the essential spiritual state nor level of being. But since they are seldom lacking in this regard, they are continually on guard, and aware, and intentional in their stations, secure in God's Care for them.

Hypocritical and pretentious people, on the other hand, have severed their communication with God. You can understand from all this why some people are in error, as well as the means by which those secure remain secure. The latter state of affairs, that is security, can come about only in that sublime state for which Servants of God are singled out and by which they become God's Friends. Know, therefore then, that spiritual state functions as the means to nearness to the Sustainer (*Rabb*) of the Universe. Look forward to ascending to this exalted station and joining the wayfarers to whom God has given His Kingdom. Once you have begun to do this, you will perceive the Truth that the only way to that state is by means of that state, and your only help towards it is in the state itself. Someone has said in this connection, "I know my Lord intimately through my Lord and were it not for my Lord I would not have known my Lord."

A story tells of how someone who asked Ali ibn Abi Talib, "Did you come to know God intimately through Muhammad or did you come to know Muhammad through God?" Ali replied, "Had I come to know God through Muhammad I would not have served God, and Muhammad would have been more firmly fixed in my soul than God. God acquainted me with Himself through Himself."

And eventually he concludes:

They endeavor to make God their Companion in all their spiritual states as much as possible. When God discerns that attitude in them He is Merciful to them by causing them to no longer rely upon their own weakness or strength in whatever they do or do not undertake, and instead He is their safeguard and protection. He guarantees their welfare and sustenance for they are His servants and are dedicated to serving Him.

There are times when we have to relate to God with the total helplessness and dependence of an infant at the mother's breast. There are moments when only that kind of companionship, complete trust and acceptance of ourselves brings the awareness that the Divine is our companion through every state. It is not to give up the practice of regular worship and *zhikr*, which is central for Sufis, but rather that we find ourselves incapable of even those basic practices that take us to the higher realms.

If we find ourselves in that state, how do we relate to God? Do we beat up on ourselves and therefore fall further back?

Mevlana says, "Adam's sin was no more than a speck of dust in his eye but it blinded him to God. It was not a big sin but his guilt over it separated him from God."

Ibn Abbad lays out all these categories of people and describes how they have some measure of self-deception or lack of self-knowledge. He offers as a remedy the "state" that will get you through this. It is only by means of the "state" that you will develop the "state." This is the same as in Ali saying "God acquainted me with Himself through Himself."

How can we come into that state? The Qur'an gives us a set of practices and rituals that are simple yet comprehensive enough to support the highest spiritual intentions.

The Qur'an says God asks the following three things of us: establish regular worship, prayer, and remembrance; give directly to those in need; and hold fast to God for He is your *Mawla*—your Friend and Protector, the One Nearest to you.

Let's start with the first one. How can we approach and benefit from *salaat*, the Islamic ritual prayer? We see *salaat* as a means of developing being and unity in our inner life. The single act of *salaat* unifies all aspects of our being. This includes the physical, emotional, mental, spiritual and unitive.

We begin *salaat* with a verbal activity, the *Fatiha*, to engage the mind. As we do so, we stand in front of Infinity. We are consciously aware of the relationship of the human to the Divine. It is a relationship of the finite to the Infinite. In the standing posture we are aware that we stand there as human beings with all the dignity of being human and of standing upright in this world. It is a very strong yet meditative position.

Next in *salaat* we bow, acknowledging our servanthood. *'Ibadah*, which means both "worship" and "servanthood," is what *salaat* is essentially. Our worship and servanthood extend to every aspect of our lives. Our worship is to be conscious of the Divine Presence and to know that our life here on earth and everything that we do becomes service when we remember God. We work, love, create, and contribute within God. We are always aware of that larger context. That is the bow of servanthood.

The next posture is the prostration. It is surrender and effacement. The forehead touches the ground. In this posture, the heart is higher than the head. This whole process of standing, bowing, and prostrating is a process of ever-deeper self-effacement. It is a process of becoming transparent to and merging with the Divine. This cycle of postures can become so whole-hearted and conscious that our normal personality and conditioned self become nonexistent because we are so present in the worship. The postures are practiced as an exercise of being.

These postures are archetypically human. We find them described in the Old Testament's *Book of Nehemiah* and also referenced in the New Testament. While the prayers are typically said in Arabic, the postures themselves existed in Judaism and Christianity. The Orthodox Church still preserves prostration as a part of worship. This kind of practice is ancient and a part of the religion of Abraham.

One of the first Qur'anic *surahs* revealed to the Prophet Muhammad describes the *musallih*, those who are worshipful. Those in remembrance, who commune with the Divine through *salaat*, are called the *saliheen*. The *salaat* referred to in Holy Scriptures before the Qur'an is different from the *salaat* as we know it.

Although today the *surah* is interpreted as referring to those who offer *salaat* and those who do not offer the ritual prayer, *salaat* had not yet been shown to the Prophet Muhammad when this verse was revealed. Muhammad learned the ritual prayer of today after his *mi'raj*, or spiritual ascent. He then taught it to his community.

The concept of *musallih* describes people who live their lives in such a way that they regularly engage in worship. There is great benefit in doing *salaat* together. In a *masjid*, a mosque, as the call to prayer is made, people who are sitting and waiting for the time to pray begin to line up. They file in and form rows. No special or privileged place is set aside for anybody. The leader of the prayer is called the *imam*. The imam has no sacramental privilege. The usefulness of an imam is in having somebody to follow in the movements and someone who can recite the Qur'an. The *salaat* can be practiced anywhere in the world by joining with others who know the format. It is a beautiful experience of bonding and human solidarity. At dawn, sunset, and night prayers, excerpts of the Qur'an are recited aloud. Upon completion of the prayer, the people will sometimes greet the person to their right and to their left and those nearby by shaking their hands and saying, "May God receive your prayer." This is a voluntary but beautiful thing to do.

There is also a blessing that can be added to the end of prayers called *Tesbihat*. This blessing was suggested by the Prophet Muhammad. It consists of saying *The Throne Verse*, reciting "*Subhanallah*" ("Glory be to God") 33 times, "*Alhamdulillah*" ("Praise be to God") 33 times, and "*Allahu Akbar*" ("God is the Greatest") 33 times. This *Tesbihat* of *Subhanallah, Alhamdulillah,* and *Allahu Akbar* was given by Prophet Muhammad to his daughter Fatima as a special gift, as related by the following story from the Tradition.

Fatima and her husband Ali were struggling in their own household at a time when the early community of believers had expanded. Ali suggested to Fatima that she go ask her father if there might be some way to assist them. Fatima went to Muhammad to ask, but then could not bring herself to make the request. She went home. Ali asked what happened. She explained. Ali said that it was OK and she should go back and just ask. Fatima went back again and she did ask. Muhammad responded that there were others who needed help more, especially the *Ahl al-Suffa*, "The People of the Bench." These were very poor people who focused directly on the Qur'an and the teachings, and who lived outside the *masjid*. Fatima went home. Later that evening Muhammad knocked and came into their little hut. They started to get up but Muhammad said, "No, stay where you are." The Prophet sat with them and asked if they would like something that would be even better. At that point, he gave them the blessing of saying 33 *Subhanallahs*, 33 *Alhamdulillahs*, and 33 *Allahu Akbars* after each ritual prayer. From that moment, Ali said, he would say that blessing after every ritual prayer for the rest of his life.

A *masjid* means a "place of prostration," coming from the root word *sajda* or "prostration." One of the beauties of this form of prayer is that it can be done in any space that we define. If we have a prayer carpet or something clean to pray on, then the whole world is our mosque and a place for prostration.

The *salaat* is a grounding exercise that helps connect us with the earth. It is a good balance to other practices that are more intoxicating and more involved with the ascent to higher planes.

At the same time, *salaat* is also called the *"miraj* of the faithful." Muhammad had his *miraj* to the infinite levels of being and to God's presence. The *salaat* is also spiritually an ascent through all the levels of being even though it is a physical act of lowering one's self onto the ground. The moment the forehead touches the earth is the high point. Mevlana says, "That moment of prostration is worth more than the Universe and all it contains."

Hearing the Music of Meaning

Resonating with the Highest Truth

WE ENCOMPASS AN INFINITE NUMBER of octaves within our being. Like a symphony orchestra, we play the music, but we should recall that there are overtones, higher octaves of meaning, as well. Can we hear or perceive that sound beyond sound? What is the highest octave?

Surah al-A'la is the chapter of "The Most High" in the Qur'an:

> *Bismillah ar-Rahman ar-Raheem*
>
> *Glorify the Name of your Sustainer the Most High who has created, and further given order and proportion, who has determined the order, and gives guidance, and who brings forth the fertile pasture, and then reduces it to darkened stubble. We shall teach you to remember so that you shall not forget except as God Wills. For truly, God knows all that is manifest and all that is hidden. And We will make easy for you the path towards true ease. So remind, in case the reminder may benefit the hearer. It will be kept in mind by those who stand in awe of God.*
>
> [*Surah al-A'la* 87:1–10]

One of the beautiful things about this teaching is its coherence, with every one of its individual parts drawing us back to the center. We are to *remind, in case the reminder may benefit the hearer.* We are our own reminder and our own hearer. To hear what is being said, we have to be in a certain state. Perhaps when we come together, silence our thoughts, still our emotions, and dedicate a little time to receptivity, we are a little more ready to hear something.

The next verse says, *Glorify the Name of your Sustainer Most High who created with order and proportion.* This orients us to the

Creative Power. It immediately gives us a sense of creation which has order and proportion. Not the least of the creation's order and proportion is the human being. That creation has the proportions of the Whole. It is a hologram of the Totality. In this sense the human being was created in the image of God.

...who has determined the order, and gives guidance, and who brings forth the fertile pasture, and then reduces it to darkened stubble. Every word is precious and if we take this to heart, it's another aspect of remembering to resonate with the Highest Truth. Why? It's that Highest Truth that determines order and gives guidance whether we recognize it or not.

Bismillah ar-Rahman ar-Raheem

Consider the Sun in its radiant brightness. And the Moon as she reflects. Consider the day as it reveals the world and the night as it veils it darkly. Consider the sky and its wondrous structure and the earth and all its expanse. Consider the human soul and the order and proportion given to it and how it is imbued with moral failings as well as with consciousness of God. Truly, the one who purifies it shall reach a happy state and the one who corrupts it shall truly be lost.

[*Surah ash-Shams* 91:1–10]

What is it that stirred Mevlana, Ibn Arabi, or any of the great masters? They were moved by, drunk on, ecstatic, humbled, and destroyed by one thing. They were in awe of and in love with one thing: the reflection of Truth in Beauty.

If we trusted the Source it came from and listened to every word of it, it would dissolve us. But a lot of the time we're not ready to hear the extraordinary Power and Truth of revelation. The Qur'an proposes that we ourselves have accumulated the rust on our hearts. It's like having stopped-up ears. Having rust on our hearts means we cannot always hear what Mevlana or the Qur'an are saying to us.

There is a story in the *Masnavi* of a man who exclaims, "Look how merciful God is! I have all these faults and I have all these sins and yet He hasn't punished me for them."

But then the Prophet Shuaib walks up to the man and says, "God wants you to know that you are wrong and that you have been punished for your sins."

The man is shocked. "Really? I have been punished for my sins? How?"

The Prophet Shuaib says to him, "Though you do your prayers, and you do them well, you do not experience their delight."

This story shows that there is "punishment" and then there is punishment.

Keeping in mind the rust on our hearts and the delight we do or do not feel in our practice… *We shall teach you to remember so that you shall not forget except as God Wills. For truly He knows all that is manifest and all that is hidden. And He will make easy for you the path towards true ease.*

Two of the most beautiful *hadiths* which are often seen in calligraphy in the East, are "Make it easy, Lord, don't make it difficult" and "We will make easy for you the path towards ultimate ease."

The Inner Ablution

It is important for us to be as free as possible from the subtle, unconscious negativity that most human beings carry around. Nobody is absolutely free of negativity. What we aim for is less negativity as we grow and mature.

The earliest teachings that we received on this Path pointed to three obstacles to spiritual progress: envy, pride, and resentment.

Envy is not like aspiration. It is not the same as wanting to be like a person who is a beautiful example. Rather, it is wanting to pull that person down, or to wish that they did not have one of their beautiful qualities. The negativity of envy is what creates an obstruction.

Pride is another subtle poison that can destroy the fruits of meditation and obstruct the flow of blessings and grace. Pride manifests in two ways. It may appear as low self-esteem and being overly critical of oneself. It may also come across as grandiosity, narcissism, or arrogance. Sometimes it may be all of those things at the same time.

Resentment, however, is the most common and destructive obstacle on the spiritual path and is a major obstacle to meditation. It creates negativity. Resentment can be quite unconscious, which makes it hard to identify.

One way we can recognize resentment is by asking ourselves if we are completely grateful in this moment. To be in a state of gratitude is to be open to Grace. We can reflect further on our gratitude to see if it includes being grateful for challenges and difficulties. When we notice our negativity, we can ask to be forgiven. We can also try to see that what we're resentful about may not be real. It may not be a complete picture we are seeing and reacting to. For example, we may experience a moment when

The Inner Ablution

we find our bosses or coworkers obnoxious, unjust, and unscrupulous. Let's say, objectively speaking, they really are that way. We can begin to use reason in this experience.

We begin by asking ourselves, "Are any of the things that bother me in the situation something that I have been guilty of?" The answer may be, "Probably." That is where we start. On the other hand, we may conclude we are blameless or that we would never have done anything similar to what the person is doing. We could still use reason by asking, "How did I get such benefits?" We probe more deeply by reflecting on why it is that we had people in our lives who provided examples of patience and unselfishness. Maybe this other person never had such models. Perhaps the person was treated cruelly and unjustly their whole life and this behavior is all they know. We can also reason by trying to pinpoint what our problems are when the person acts this way. We can ask ourselves how the behavior is hurting us. What are we afraid of? What are our insecurities? And finally, we may ask ourselves, "What good does it do me to be resentful? Why am I accepting this toxin into my system?"

The Qur'an talks about resentment in *Surah al-A'raf*.

> *But those who attain to faith and do righteous deeds— [and] We do not burden any human being more than he is well able to bear—they are destined for paradise therein to abide, after We shall have removed whatever unworthy thoughts or feelings may have been [lingering] in their bosoms. Running waters will flow at their feet, and they will say all praise is due to God who has guided us onto this for we certainly would not have found the right path unless God had guided us. Indeed our Sustainer's apostles have told us the truth. And a voice will call out to them, "This is the paradise that you have inherited by virtue of your past deeds."*
>
> [*Surah al-A'raf* 7:42–43, trans. Muhammad Asad]

This passage conveys an incredible promise. It is addressed to those who have faith and do *salahat*, the work of reconciliation. The message is that something is required of us. *Salahat* implies reconciliation and the overcoming of resentment. The neutralization of negativity occurs only with God's help. When you see the neutralization happening you typically reciprocate with love. You freely begin to do more of what has brought about the spiritual progress you've experienced. This allows God's help to arrive regularly.

The messages in *Surah al-A'raf* are a beautiful example of the simplicity and importance of what is revealed in the Qur'an. The *unworthy thoughts or feelings* that *may have been lingering in their bosoms* refer to whatever resentment may have been in the heart. *Running waters will flow at their feet* tells us there will be greater ease and fluidity in us when resentment is gone. It is like being in a state of paradise or among beautiful springs in a desert oasis. When the heart is free of resentment, something begins to flow.

On the Sufi path a person ideally offers the ritual prayer five times each day. Before doing the ritual prayer, one performs ablutions: a ritual washing with water of the hands, lower arms, mouth, nostrils, face, ears, neck, and feet. In Arabic, ablution is called *wudu* and it is done after one goes to the bathroom, sleeps, or if there is any kind of emission of bodily fluid.

In Sufism, one always tries to be in a state of ablution, and so one is always ready to pray. Most people know about ablutions as the outward form of washing. A fewer number know there is also an inner ablution.

Outer ablutions purify us at the physical, hygienic, and electromagnetic levels. The outer ablution cleanses our senses and readies the body for prayer and worship. The inner ablution helps ready our heart for prayer and worship. Ablution allows us to come into God's presence and to feel we have a right to be there. We can be in God's presence not because we are perfect, but in spite of our imperfections. The following prayer is called "The Inner Ablution":

As long as I embodied in this world, I am not perfect.
I am capable of mistakes, faults, and wrongs.

The Inner Ablution

> I take refuge in the love of our Sustainer and humbly beg forgiveness.
> I ask forgiveness of anyone I have wronged
> and in the same spirit I forgive those who have wronged me
> because I wish to love them as God loves them.
> Being convinced of the sincerity of my repentance
> I feel cleansed, purified and free of any pain, resentment, or guilt
> and gratefully assume my rightful place in God's presence.

The inner ablution has goals we may feel we cannot reach right now. However, affirming what appears out of reach helps convince the subconscious mind it is possible. The Divine wishes us to be in our rightful place before It. We can do this by stepping into that state that the inner ablution call us to. We are invited to the goals of inner ablution whether we feel completely ready or not. Making an inner ablution may help us see that perhaps we have not forgiven someone. We may realize that our sincerity is fleeting. We may feel inappropriate in asking for forgiveness. Inner ablution can help us assess where we are on a continuum of sincerity and repentance.

The first line of "The Inner Ablution" is a recognition of our imperfection. It reminds us that imperfection is not failure. Some degree of imperfection will continue as long as we are embodied. We should keep up our efforts knowing that perfection is not the goal. Constantly returning to ask for forgiveness is the goal.

"The Inner Ablution" has nine lines. In numerology, nine is the number of cycles it takes to reach completion. This number of lines implies that those who do inner ablution do so to begin and continue the cycle again. As we assume our rightful place in God's presence, we go on with our life. We begin in a fresh state, knowing we will be returning to the process of forgiving and seeking forgiveness.

Rumi's *Masnavi* tells us we can ask for forgiveness even if we don't see or understand the connection between what we may have done and how it may be making us feel. There is a passage in the *Masnavi* that describes how a baby was created by sperm. The sperm was created by a man's body. The man's body used food to create the sperm. There are causal links among the baby, the sperm, and the food, but you don't always think of them because they are subtle. Mevlana suggests we examine what action might be related to the pain or sadness we may be feeling because the connections there may also be subtle. Most of the time we may not be able to pinpoint what it is that precipitated our pain or sadness. This is where we can use meditation and contemplation to ask God for knowledge, help, and forgiveness. God's mercy is infinitely generous. God can answer even a distracted, superficial, or general prayer for help and forgiveness. We may find God's mercy arrives, even when we pray while in a distressed or unknowing state.

The person who can enter a state of pure being through meditation and contemplation can recognize the need to call on God when it arises. Such a person unites reason with the subconscious faculties of the heart. This opens a person up, potentially, to knowledge and perception as she sees God's answers to her questions and responses to her requests. Meditation and contemplation create a gathered and present state in which we can commune with the Divine as a mature person. Regular outer and inner ablutions facilitate presence. Greater coherence and more awakened faculties can result. This, in turn, can bring more precise and clear communication with the Divine.

There are connections between *Surah al-A'raf* and the inner ablution. When we pray in "The Inner Ablution" that it is our desire to love others as God loves them, our perspective shifts from the "I" of the *nafs* to the "I" of the heart. *Surah al-A'raf* tells us that God will not burden any creature with more than he or she can bear. Knowing this helps us maintain a heart-based perspective, allowing grace and support to flow into us.

When we prostrate, our hearts are higher than our head. In prostration, we can humbly ask forgiveness. A realignment of our

The Inner Ablution

being occurs naturally when we prostrate and seek forgiveness. Prostrating provides relief from burdens. The feeling of ease and of being cleansed serves as an incentive to continue to seek forgiveness. When you welcome prostration and reconciliation, you experience life as a garden. Grace and realignment return swiftly and continuously. They remain longer. This is a gift from God.

In Sufism, we learn that the virtues of love, compassion, mercy, patience, forgiveness, conscience, and remorse can neutralize some of the negativities that obstruct the flow of Grace.

Real change requires we feel remorse when it is appropriate. We may be reluctant to view remorse as something that can bring us into light. Yet remorse is different from neurotic guilt, compulsively blaming ourselves, focusing on our imperfections, or otherwise experiencing what is commonly known as "shame." Remorse can be helpful if it accompanies a moment of waking up to something that we really need to see and change. Remorse in this context is tempered by modesty and deep humility.

We can feel remorse and even revulsion when we see we have damaged our own humanness. We damage our humanness when we are doing something that is contrary to our nature. Our nature is pure. A healthy remorse arises when we recognize our negativity. We may see that we have been cruel, selfish, and unconscious. We thank God for letting us see this. Our remorse in that moment becomes a blessing. It's okay if such recognition hurts. To suffer with such a moment is appropriate if the suffering continues to a productive point.

If we make too much of our sins, it's egoism. Perseverating about a failure we have seen in ourselves is a denial of God's Grace. It is not that important that we have blocked God's Grace by feeling resentment. If resentment goes unrecognized and becomes a tone in our everyday life, it is damaging to our souls.

Our aim is to purify our heart and to be open to communion with the Divine. This brings joy and light into our lives. Grace and realignment enhance our ability to get along well with others. Inner ablution can lead to deeper bonds with others. We grow into a true spiritual community by practicing the fruits of love. These include the qualities of kindness, humbleness, guilelessness, patience, forgiveness, endurance, cheerfulness, encouragement, courtesy, unselfishness, courage, and keeping our word.

Humbleness, gratitude, and love can serve us as a means to break through the obstacles that envy, resentment, and pride create. Humbleness shatters pride. Gratitude counters resentment. Love dissipates envy. Humbleness, gratitude, and love are keys to opening the flow of Grace. We feel joy, light, compassion, and gratitude in our being as individuals and in community with the wayfarers of the Way, the lovers of God.

Offering the Heart, Levels of Purification

Water says to the dirty one, "Come."
The dirty one says, "But, I'm so ashamed."
Water says, "But how will you become clean without me?"

[*Masnavi* II, 1366–67]

SUFISM IS A PRACTICE AND PROCESS for taking us beyond the limitations of the thinking mind and habitual emotions. As a habitual "I," we live in a construct of our thoughts and what our parents or society told us we are. We project into the future, remember the past, judge ourselves, blame ourselves, and experience inner contradictions. Such a life reflects all the images, messages, and resulting emotions that come from the media and that are manufactured by commercial, political, and falsely religious institutions. Being bombarded with images and messages allows these institutions to control and manipulate us. How will the soul withstand and know itself apart from all of this? How can it do so, withstand and know itself while not reacting to all of this and saying it's bad?

The verse by Mevlana about water and the dirty one present a beautifully vivid metaphor for this dilemma. On one side, we have our human condition, our egoism, our self-denigration, our shame, our guilt. Then, we're told about Water that cleanses. This is the Water of Reality, Life, Grace, and Mercy. With an idea like this entering deep enough into our hearts, whole layers of shame and negativity may be washed away.

Once we step outside of the thinking mind and the reactive and contradictory emotions, we move into another dimension of our soul. Cultivating that with a gentle discipline, moment by moment, day by day, and year by year, we begin to live in that state constantly. Then, ideally *what is* is what is. With this practice, we learn to trust Reality. We learn not to fantasize about and create a false reality or a false self. There is this possibility of awakening a pure state of being that simply is. By doing so, we experience a state of being that is our self and not a construct of the mind. This state of being is pure witnessing that is guided by and informed by a greater Intelligence.

And so we can develop a capacity of being that experiences itself as a reflection of greater Being. As such, we can be one with a wider field of Being, and yet remain individualized. We have a self that can be responsible and functional while also maintaining relationships.

This process of inner ablution takes on an additional dimension through interaction with others. In the words of the Prophet Muhammad: "Two believers that lend support to each other are like a pair of hands that wash each other clean." Our friendship and support of our friends is no different than hands washing each other because of the unity and co-operation involved.

It is also said that a prophet cleanses his community as if it were his own body. The power of a great spiritual figure's being extends far beyond their individuality and brings coherence and harmony to a community, a whole nation, and centuries of souls. That is the nature of the soul when it is in communion with Reality and the Universe of Grace.

To be a friend of God, or *wali* in Arabic, is to be near to God who is also the ultimate *Wali*. We may strive to be His friend but He already is our Friend. The Grace and Beneficence of the Divine Friend, *al-Wali*, the Divine Supporter, is manifested in all of existence. It includes all the beautiful qualities of human nature, the presence of guidance and prophethood throughout history, and also the tests we face in life. With enough experience and maturity, we realize that even hardships are signs of the guidance and benevolence of the Friend, *al-Wali*.

There is a beautiful eleventh-century description of *awliyah* from Khwajah Abdullah Ansari of Herat, Afghanistan, written about 1,000 years ago:

> The Friends of God are divers for pearls of wisdom in the oceans of the sciences of Reality. They are the sign of devotion in the heavens of primordial human nature that is established permanently in the testament of Divine Favor, honored in God's Presence, treasures of Divine Mysteries super-scribed by the law, being themselves the demonstration of Divine Reality. The lineage of Muhammad in the realm of spiritual truths is resuscitated through them. The way of righteousness is constant through their firm-footedness. Their outward character is adorned with moral principles, their inner being illuminated with the luminous jewel of spiritual poverty. The sign of the Friend of God is that he or she is the very substance of holy reverence from head to foot. His or her eyes are as if they were painted with reverence so that he or she does not gaze on anything improper. That one's tongue is fettered by courtesy so that he or she never speaks a frivolous word. His or her foot is shackled by Divine Reality so that he or she does not wantonly go about to court each place or fortune. His or her limbs are bound by the bonds of servitude so that he or she does not gird his or her loins except in the service of Truth.

As with all friendships, our friendship with God also has two dimensions. One way is with the Divine being near to us, and the other is the possibility of intentionally and consciously drawing near to the Divine. But in both cases the process is aided by emptying ourselves, rather than by pouring lots of information into ourselves.

Even if it is the knowledge from the mystics, filling ourselves only with such concepts would have us be, as Mevlana Rumi says, "… a donkey with a big load of books on our backs." The value of their words is not as information to retain in our memory but rather in the effect they have on our perception.

The real process is to take that knowledge and let it open us to the realities the language is speaking about. As an example, a few words as simple as, *Indeed in the remembrance of God, hearts find rest,*[35] offer a huge amount of knowledge and guidance. These few simple words make up one of the most valuable concepts a human being could possibly receive.

If we were sincere, a little would take us a long way. A page or two of Mevlana or of the Qur'an is more than enough to carry a human being very far. The key is having the right learning attitude and avoiding being a mere passive consumer of information. In short, it is important to take what we read and hear to heart, by stepping out of our habitual thoughts and feelings. We can open pure-heartedly to simply what is. We can cleanse our hearts and minds to open up to this possibility and state. We can see how the heart already belongs to God.

---

35. Surah ar-Ra'd 13:28.

Humbleness, Gratitude, Love

THE SUFIS SEE THE HEART as having the only true intelligence. Our task is to educate the heart with inner and outer disciplines. The most important is *zhikr Allah*. In the morning the *faqir*, the indigent beggar before God, wakes up, takes out the *tesbih*,[36] and begins to give attention to the Divine, saying "Allah! Allah! Allah!"

The intention is simply to be present with every "Allah." Imagine going through the prayer beads simply saying "Allah" and knowing when we are saying "Allah" we mean the Absolute Divine Reality. It is not an abstract activity. We are remembering total Oneness, the Inner, the Outer, the First, the Last, the Origin of our consciousness, and the Source of love and forgiveness.

Bead by bead, while we say "Allah, Allah, Allah," the heart is just watching "Allah, Allah, Allah." For some time we may only get so far in this practice before we have runaway thoughts. Eventually, though, with work, dedication, and practice, it becomes possible to be present for the whole prayer bead cycle. If we keep coming back to this practice, over time the "eye of the heart" becomes a watcher of those runaway thoughts and brings them back. We learn to become a watcher over our mind and a gatekeeper of our hearts. In time, and even without prayer beads, we learn to pay attention to the quality and content of our thoughts and to watch our emotional reactions if they appear in the form of judgments, resentments, and jealousy. With this practice we begin to have the capacity to notice these things.

In this process, it eventually becomes possible to summon the beautiful qualities of humbleness, gratitude, and love as well as to be open to the inflow of Divine Being.

---

36. Prayer beads.

There was once a dervish who was suffering with a horrible toothache. A day came when he was relieved of his suffering and he started asking everybody he knew if they were happy. Most of the people he met were not happy. They related innumerable negativities, resentments, and complaints against life. He said to them, "But you don't have a toothache! Why aren't you happy? You should be happy!" Gratitude can begin with noticing all the little things we might otherwise take for granted.

Humbleness is knowing our dependence on the Divine and our interdependence with our fellow human beings, especially our spiritual family. Humbleness is also the ability to say to the Universe, "I'm sorry. Forgive me." We apologize for every judgment that arises, every complaint we have, and every minuscule motion toward blame. We notice these things with remembrance, presence, and gratitude.

Humility reminds and enables us to ask for forgiveness for whatever arises on the screen of our consciousness in the form of judging, complaining, resenting, being jealous, or being angry. This isn't just about us. The whole of Reality is interconnected with a non-causal relationship among all its parts. Every one of us has the capacity to transform and heal the whole by simply doing the inner work. It is humbly saying, "I'm sorry," and asking forgiveness of the Universe for blaming someone for doing something different than how we would do it.

The mystics tell us there is something truly extraordinary going on here. Every human being who is relatively conscious has the capacity to purify and transform whatever comes into their awareness. We have a responsibility towards our communities to sustain a state that is positive, wise, forgiving, loving, hopeful, and aware of God. We are hopeful under all the conditions in which we live. We move in the direction of greater human equality and dignity. We aspire to greater mutual understanding and love. We are all one human family struggling on the Path. We came from one Soul, one Mother. We can take every difficult, negative, problematic moment arising within our souls and transform it with love.

Humbleness, Gratitude, and Love

The Qur'an says, *Respond to evil with what is most beautiful.*[37] We have the capacity to respond to evil with something beautiful.

Our practice of *La ilaha il Allah*[38] is an emptying of ourselves of our idols of self-importance, and of our egoistic vantage points that usually result in judgment, blame, complaint, fear, jealousy, and loss of hope.

Day after day, we keep coming back to beads, breaths, humility, gratitude, and love. We learn more and more to live in this spacious reality and state of remembrance (*zhikr*).

There are three levels of understanding *zhikr*. The first level comes to us from the Qur'an. The Qur'an says, *Zhikr is the greatest.*[39] It is the greatest of anything and everything. The simplest, most direct way to be in remembrance is through a Divine Name. Surah al-Muzzammil says, *Remember the Name of your Lord, the Sustainer, and devote yourself wholeheartedly to God, the Only Divinity, Lord of the rising and the setting sun, the Only Disposer of your affairs.*[40]

The *surah* says *devote yourself wholeheartedly*. We are being told that we are to give ourselves completely to the one and only Divinity. The *surah's* original language referring to Allah as the Lord of the rising and the setting sun can also be translated as *Lord of the East and the West*. The East is where the sun rises and the West is where it sets. We typically forget that the Arabic words for "East" and "West" derive from words referring to the *direction* of sunrise and sunset. Keeping the root meaning in mind, we can understand this *surah* to be referring us to that one Divinity who is the One that brings forth and settles the Light.

The *surah* tells us that God is the only disposer of our affairs. He is the only *Wakil*, which is one of the names of God in the Qur'an. God is the only one that is Absolutely Trustworthy. He is the Trustee. Remembering God by His Names within the context taught by *Surah al-Muzzammil* is the first level of remembrance.

---

37. Surah Fussilat 41:34.
38. There is no god but God.
39. Surah al-'Ankabut 29:45.
40. Surah al-Muzzammil 73:8–9.

The second level of *zhikr* is the stage of remembering the Sacred Divine Essence more deeply and within our hearts. The Qur'an says, *Remember your Lord, your Sustainer, within yourself.*[41]

How do we follow this advice? We do so humbly, reverently, with awe, and even with a little bit of trepidation because this undertaking is extremely important. Don't ever take the words *within yourself* in this passage from the Qur'an for granted. The guidance really does mean *within*. But it does not mean "in your head," or "in your thoughts." We are told, *Remember your Lord, your Sustainer, within yourself in the mornings and the evenings and do not be heedless.* Heedless in Arabic is *ghaflah* and has the meaning of being unconscious, or foolishly oblivious.

The third stage of *zhikr*, the ultimate level, is when a person ascends higher than just performing the remembrance of God. We pass beyond remembering the Divine within our hearts and arrive at a state of remembrance where the characteristics of beauty, richness, and essence of the Divine reflect in us and through us. *Surah al-Ahzab* tells us: *O you who have true faith, remember God, remember much, and glorify God morning and evening.*[42]

In the third stage, there's remembrance of the tongue, the heart, and in action. It's possible that a human being can be in such a state of remembrance that every movement and all that is said continuously reflects the Divine.

These three stages are not linear. One does not go from one stage to the next or forever stay at a particular stage.

This knowledge from revelation is a beautiful reminder of what a human being is capable of experiencing in active relationship with God. This is the most basic teaching of our Path. It is also the highest teaching. Living this teaching takes up our whole spiritual journey. There's nothing more basic and simple than remembering God. We, human beings, can experience the illumination from the Cosmic Essence because of the nature of our souls and hearts. A person's spiritual substance and nature

---

41. Surah al-A'raf 7:205.
42. Surah al-Ahzab 33: 41–42.

can turn sincerely towards the Divine Source. Such a turning can vibrationally attune a person into that Reality. This, in turn, renews the resonance so that a person's self, mind, emotions, body, actions, and behaviors will be transformed. The connection and relationship is a vibrational linkage, a channel, and a broadcast of very real energy. However, if we're living among the heedless we are very likely oblivious to the connection and what is being continuously transmitted through it.

Remembrance is more than just a repetitive mouthing of words. If we're in remembrance we are conscious of every step. In *zhikr*, we know what is right and appropriate in every moment. It is as if we were in the sight of God. In *zhikr*, there is a real sense of knowing we are in a Divine Reality. We want to conduct ourselves in the most beautiful ways because we're in the vision of that beauty.

It is left to us to do this practice of *zhikr* and to awaken the heart so that it is capable of living more and more in a state linked to the Divine. *Zhikr* is not a mental procedure or a technical way to experience a state of bliss. Ultimately, *zhikr* rules what we do, how we do it, how we act, how aware we are of spiritual laws, and how we accord ourselves with the highest ethics we know. Remembrance is always raising us to a higher level of kindness, generosity, honesty, courage, and justice.

What Does it Mean to Be a Dervish?

*D*ervish is a Persian word suggesting a *threshold*. It is a threshold between the finite and the Infinite, or the physical and the spiritual. The heart of the human being is the threshold where these two worlds meet. One of the first things we are taught on this Path is that a dervish is one who stands at the threshold between slavery and freedom. That is the ideal.

One of the things that characterizes a dervish is a willingness to not be governed or ruled by the *nafs* (false self). A dervish does not let the *nafs* be the decider.

On our Path we are very compassionate towards the lower self and treat it with respect, but Spirit rules. The higher self rules to the extent that Spirit can awaken, be present, and take its rightful authority with the *nafs* as a servant. The lower self has its rights. We honor those rights. We allow it some pleasures and satisfactions, but not all. And we certainly do not allow it the unjust, unethical, or wrong kind of ambitions. We do not allow it to manifest in jealousy, envy, pride, or arrogance. The dervish is someone who makes a practice of humility, service, friendship, loyalty, and patience, as the following story illustrates:

There was once a shaikh in Ottoman times who supposedly had 100,000 dervishes. The sultan was warned about this shaikh by his viziers. They said to him, "This man is getting too powerful. We better do something because he has got so many dervishes, and dervishes are crazy people who will do anything." The sultan called in this shaikh and said, "Baba, how many dervishes do you have?" The shaikh replied, "One and a half." "We hear you have 100,000 dervishes," responded the sultan. "No, no, I only have one and a half," replied the shaikh. The sultan said, "I don't believe you. Tomorrow we will call all of your dervishes to meet outside the city on the plain near the hills. Everyone who considers themselves a dervish of yours we want to see there tomorrow."

The next day the sultan set up a big tent on the plain near the hills. Thousands upon thousands of people turned up. All of them claimed to be dervishes of the shaikh. It was then announced, "We need ten dervishes to sacrifice their lives for the life of the shaikh. If we can find ten of you to sacrifice your lives, then we will spare him."

One man's hand went up and he said, "My shaikh has taught me everything I know. I would willingly give my life for him." This man was summoned and taken into the tent. After a short while everyone heard the sound of chopping and saw blood coming from underneath the tent. Another announcement was made, "Are there any other dervishes of this shaikh here?" An old woman raised her hand. She was summoned and taken into the tent. After a short while everyone again heard the sound of chopping and saw more blood coming from underneath the tent. Another announcement was made, "Is anybody else here a dervish of this shaikh?" Slowly everybody turned around and started walking away. Nobody knew it had been sheep that had been slaughtered in the tent instead of the dervishes.

Then the sultan and the viziers came to the shaikh and said, "You said you had one and a half dervishes. So you had this man and this woman who was the half dervish." The shaikh replied, "No, no, you have it backwards. The man is the half dervish because when he volunteered he didn't know for sure whether he would die. My only full dervish is that woman because when she volunteered she was sure she would die."

A dervish lives in trust, not fear. Dervishhood prepares us for the trials and sufferings of this life, and equally prepares us for the next life.

The dervish is completely integrated with life while remembering God and being thankful with every breath. Ideally a dervish would have a socially productive livelihood and, if it be so destined, be married with children while living in community. Although living an exceptional life in some ways, a dervish does not require withdrawal from society and earns his own bread. When the Ottoman sultans became Mevlevi dervishes, their shaikhs told them to learn a trade. Even Sultan Selim III, a great Mevlevi dervish, who was sultan during one of the highest periods of the Ottoman Empire, had to learn calligraphy and sell his work to earn his bread. Humility is characteristic of dervishhood.

Once there was a dervish named Abdul Majeed. When returning from Mecca he passed a child playing in the sand. Abdul Majeed stopped and watched this child. Over and over, the child would build beautiful pyramids, only to knock them over and cry. Abdul Majeed asked the child, "What are you doing?" The child looked at him and said, "Abdul Majeed! I am doing what people do!" Abdul Majeed was surprised and asked, "How did you know my name and why do you do this?" The child said, "When I build these beautiful pyramids of sand I am doing the work of uniting hearts. When I destroy them I am doing what people do to break hearts. It makes me weep when hearts are broken." Abdul Majeed knew there was deep meaning in what he had heard and asked the child if he could stay and be his student. A dervish is willing to learn, even from a child.

In the Qur'an, God says, *We will show them our signs on the farthest horizons and within themselves until they know the Truth.*[43] It is through that continual manifesting of signs that we are in communication with the Divine.

The spiritual work is all about actualizing communication with the Divine, which can be through prayer, art, dance, music, or any other genuine expression. The day-to-day work of the dervish is inner mastery by holding and falling in love with Beauty. This is so much easier than trying to be non-judgmental. Every thought can be communication with the Divine to the extent that it is conscious. The work of a dervish is to increase the capacity

---

43. *Surah Fussilat* 41:53.

to communicate with the Creative Spirit. The reality of that covers every manifestation and condition of life. Our communication with the Divine can be developed in a conscious process that includes prayer, intention, and an emptying of self.

We become and are imbued with the fragrance of whatever we hold in the space of our hearts. We can hold continual gratitude, trust, and humility with the awareness of our dependence on the One. We can be in continual non-blame. For the Sufi, the intention is to be in continual glorification. That glorification arises from remembering and recognizing the beauty, power, and glory of the Divine.

Mevlana tells us: "If your thought is a rose, then you are the Rose Garden. If your thought is a thorn, then you are just kindling for the bath-stove" (*Masnavi* II, 278).

I recall chopping wood with an elderly dervish once. It was an almost painful experience to stand next to him because it was like being in front of a highly polished mirror in whose presence everything became clear. A dervish is that kind of *mum'in*, or believer. One of the purposes of coming together is to be with others who will reflect ourselves back to us and help us to see and know ourselves better. It is possible to be with people with whom we cozily daydream and who help to justify our weaknesses and who reassure us that we need not aspire to very much. Aspiring in the most real sense can make things uncomfortable. A real dervish is one who helps us improve ourselves.

A sultan and his advisor went on a journey. On the way, the sultan saw two people with huge stacks of wood on their backs talking to each other intently. The sultan continued on his way. Several hours later, the sultan returned to the area. He saw the same two people still there talking, each still holding their huge stack of wood on his back. The sultan asked, "Who are these people?" His advisor answered, "They are dervishes. When they come together, they forget about their burdens."

One of the Prophet Muhammad's beautiful sayings is: "The *mum'in* is a mirror to the *mum'in*." Or, "The believer is a mirror to the believer." The *mum'in* is someone who has reached certainty regarding spiritual dimensions as well as the beneficence of the Unseen. The *mum'in* has come to a real faith and certainty about the presence, purpose, and meaning of life by knowing and experiencing the spiritual dimension beyond appearances. The believer is the best mirror there is.

In Konya, during Rumi's time, a person once went to his son Sultan Veled and asked, "May I become your dervish?" Sultan Veled said, "I cannot accept you." The person left and travelled all the way up to Ankara. There he came into the presence of Haji Bayram Veli. The person said, "Baba, will you receive me as your dervish?" Haji Bayram Veli said, "*Eyvallah*." Some time later, this person travelled back to Konya and went to visit Sultan Veled. When he found Sultan Veled the person told him, "You would not receive me as a dervish but Haji Bayram Veli has accepted me." Sultan Veled responded, "Haji Bayram Veli is a vast Ocean and it does not matter what you drop into that Ocean." The dervish returned to Ankara and to Haji Bayram Veli. He said, "When I went to Sultan Veled and told him you had accepted me as a dervish, he said you are a vast Ocean and it does not matter who you throw into that Ocean because it is vast enough to accommodate anyone. I am so happy a great shaikh like you accepted me and he did not." Haji Bayram Veli responded, "Do you know why Sultan Veled did not accept you? Sultan Veled is like a pail of the purest milk. If you were to drop in a single eyelash, you would notice it."

Stories like this also reveal the importance of *adab* in our Tradition. When we first came to the Path, we spent some time in the company of some dervishes of other orders. We were stunned by something we sensed which we could not quite identify. It was the quality of dervishhood.

On one hand, the word dervish implies humility. Dervishes are humble and loving even to those they do not know. They are devoted, kind, and strong with each other. One feels dervishes are a group of human beings that are unified in a way that is quite remarkable.

At the same time, the dervish sees with two "eyes" or perspectives. The eye of *wahdat* looks out at the world with no judgments. Sufis in a state of *wahdat* look outwards and have no complaints against God. They see the perfection of everything as it is. It does not mean they see saint and sinner as well as justice and injustice as equal. They see the differences and contradictions, but also see their perfection and usefulness in the beautiful state of *wahdat*. If there is an injustice, the dervish will try to make it right while still seeing the perfection of the Oneness.

The other "eye" or perspective is one of discernment. A dervish also sees within herself objectively, and recognizes the better and the worse. She sees the things that need improvement and the work that needs doing. The dervish has a healthy sense of self-criticism.

The Malamati, for example, are a community of Sufis known as the people on the path of blame. They are visible to others with their outer lives, but invisible with their inner life. They don't wear their spirituality on their sleeve. They even court a little bit of disapproval because they feel that is healthy for the ego. The path of blame directly confronts the need to look good or win approval.

What makes us self-conscious and fearing to be judged? Every human being wants positive regard and to be loved. We once asked a respected spiritual teacher if we ever reach a point where we no longer feel we need to be loved. Without hesitation, he said, "Yes. When you love."

The fruits of love include patience, forgiveness, generosity, kindness, equanimity, compassion, gratitude, guilelessness, and humility. The tree of love will produce these fruits. At the same time, these fruits produce the tree of love. We can awaken any one of these fruits of love with the cause producing the effect and the effect producing the cause.

The dervish is aspiring to that state of loving all creatures because of the love of the Creator and serving everything that is good. The Prophet Muhammad (peace be upon him) is an exemplar of being in love with the Formless and at the same time living a very practical life. One of the characteristics of the Sufi tradition is the integration of the teachings with everyday life.

The servants of the Infinitely Compassionate walk humbly on the earth, and when the ignorant accost them, their only reply is "Peace".[44] In our spiritual universe, the Divine Teacher and Guide is bringing down Words. Jesus was a "Word of God." Each of us is also a Word and governed by a Divine Name. Our possibilities in life are realized through our characteristic Divine Quality.

In the Qur'an, God says, *The Word of your Sustainer is fulfilled in truth and in justice.*[45] It's a powerful statement signifying the Word as one of the foremost creative ways the human manifests the Divine. The Truth of these revelations is fulfilled in life on earth and in living in justice.

There is no true justice without mercy. Mercy precedes everything, and it is why we are here. Mercy created us and is what is being revealed. The dervish dispenses, communicates, and shares that mercy. Sometimes wrath may be mixed in, but it is always in the service of mercy. God said to the Prophet, "We sent you only as a mercy to the Worlds."

The dervish is one who is merciful.

In Konya, over the entryway to the *dergah* where Mevlana is buried, is an inscription which says, "This is the Kaaba of the Lovers. Those who entered here became complete." The dervish walks the Path of completion.

A Sufi has complete integration with life while remembering God with every breath. The great majority of Sufis have lived a family life, held a job, and contributed to society, while reaching extraordinary attainments of integrating the finite and the Infinite. They lived in a state of *wahdat*.

---

44. Surah al-Furqan 25:63.
45. Surah al-An'am 6:115.

Reflections on Suleyman Dede, an Ocean of Love

THE FIRST TIME WE MET Suleyman Hayati Dede at the Claymont Society in West Virginia, we were trying to understand what it was about Dede that was different compared to the other sincere and eminent teachers we had met. Some of these masters had worked on themselves their whole lives. What was it that made Dede so exceptional? It wasn't that he had anything extraordinary to say; his teachings were really quite simple. It was something subtle yet powerful.

On reflection, it was that in Dede there was no self-assertion whatsoever. Dede did take strong action from time to time, but the person receiving the roasting would feel it was not coming from Dede's own personality, and in some way I suspect they knew they deserved it. They might be humiliated but also very grateful because it came from love. Some teachers are quite powerful, knowledgeable, and channel a lot of force. But it was truly rare for us to have met somebody who was transparent and without any self-assertion.

Suleyman Dede was someone who spoke from a place of deep knowing, a place much greater than himself. Suleyman Dede was not just an individual while speaking. He was representing something Infinite. The love, acceptance, and belonging you felt from him made you want to be with him for the rest of your life. It made you want to never leave his side. Some said that in Suleyman Dede's embrace you felt as though you were in your mother's arms. You felt a real sense of being in a state beyond comparing, free from like or dislike.

Suleyman Dede spoke with the genuine voice of the Prophet Muhammad. The love he gave came from a deep center within his heart. His heart was connected to Mevlana Rumi, and the Prophet. He was part of something that was intricately and carefully balanced. Suleyman Dede said chance did not play a role in the people he met. He knew that wherever he was, it was the right place, right time, and that he had been called for a specific service. He was awake to that.

Dede said that we are never separated from God. He invited us to enter into the experience described by *Surah al-Hadid*: *He is with you wherever you are*.[46]

Knowing that God is very close to us creates the longing to get closer still. There is this force and power that keeps pulling us. It increases the longing in our hearts and the taste of knowing that God is near.

---

46. *Surah al-Hadid* 57:4.

The Drop That Knows

SUFI METAPHYSICS IS SOMETIMES expressed through poetry. The great thirteenth-century shepherd-poet Yunus Emre—the greatest Turkish-language poet who ever lived—spoke of the "drop that *contains* the Ocean," not the drop that *dissolves* in the Ocean.

Today, it's easy to understand this expression because we have holograms. A hologram of the portion can reflect the whole. In Sufi metaphysics we have so many things that point to this. In our Tradition, God says, "The heavens and the earth cannot contain Me." We know there are billions of stars and galaxies. Yet the Divine is saying, "No, all of that cannot contain Me. Only the heart of my faithful servant, the knower, is expansive enough to contain Me." It's a very high truth.

A drop that knows itself, knows the Ocean. In a way it's very simple. All of the qualities, energies, capacities, and functions that are in the human being—such as consciousness, love, and will—do not originate in this physical organism. All of these things and more are sourced in Divine Reality. They are sourced in God. Things that arise within us are attributes of the Divine. They are attributes of the Source and are given to the human being. Everything that we are is of that Ocean. We are the drops, but our consciousness, our love, our will, is of that Ocean.

The work of spirituality is to activate the Divine Attributes in ourselves. Everything that we do is to clear away what obstructs that activation. We are trying to open up the aperture of Divine Awareness and remove what is blocking it. We call upon that Source to activate Itself through us. Prayer, worship, supplication, contemplation, meditation, and glorification polish the mirror to improve what the human being can reflect.

If you enter dervishhood and do this seriously, you short-circuit all of the ploys of the false self, such as trying to gain attention, not wanting to be ignored, trying to gain approval, maximizing pleasure and security, and avoiding pain and insecurity.

A dervish has yoked himself or herself to the cart of servanthood. The dervish chooses courage in the face of fear. The dervish uses fear and threatening things as an opportunity to summon courage. The dervish expects to face difficulties. Mevlana says, "Pure gold delights in the fire." It's only in the fire that gold proves it is gold and all the dross burns away. Elsewhere Mevlana says, "Embrace insecurity, be at home amidst dangers." Yunus Emre says, "Sip the poison, give the sweet drink to others."

Only this pure, objective witness inside ourselves—the awakened "I"—has the capacity to relate to God. Only with an awakened "I" do we have the possibility of true relationship with the Divine. One of our teachers said, "There is no God, unless I am." This is a little variation on *La ilaha il Allah*, "There is no god but God." What a pleasure it is to be aware, in any moment, while doing the simple things. What a joy it is to be aware for no other reason than to be aware, and to be grateful that's possible. The Divine has given us this awareness, sourced in the Source.

The awakened "I" experiences itself in a world made up of this moment of existence. It experiences what is, and is grateful and appreciative for what is. The dervish is grateful and appreciative, no matter what. Being in this state doesn't keep us from working to improve things. We always begin with appreciating and being grateful for what is. If we feel a need, we invoke the Divine for what we truly need, not what we want. We should always ask the Divine for something higher, something better, in spiritual terms. We should try to always aim and choose the higher, even if there's risk involved.

It's okay if you fail. If you do fail, you choose again. You choose what is higher, better, and more Godly each time. You choose what is more conscious and more holy. For us, holy does not mean some false piety. All life is one and everything that lives is holy. Holiness is Reality.

"The drop that knows Itself knows the Ocean." You are the Ocean. You are potentially the drop containing all the qualities of God. In our Tradition, the first thing the Divine gave to the primordial human being, Adam, was a consciousness of the Divine Names. The Divine Names are the creative powers of existence and the Universe. Ninety-nine of these Names are known explicitly in our Tradition. In reality, they are an infinite number in their manifestation. Every attribute of the Divine is in every human being, whether they're awakened or not. The attributes may be in a latent state, where very little is called forth, but they are there. The complete human being, the *insan al-kamil*, is the activation of the full spectrum of Divine Qualities. The spectrum includes everything from Absolute Gentleness to Absolute Power, from Mercy to Strength, and from Subtlety to Clarity. It includes *Haqq* or Truth. This is our orientation on the spiritual path.

All of our practices are for removing what obstructs this activation. The aim is to increase our quality of being so that we can observe the false self, have the knowledge to re-educate and recondition it, and to have the power of observation and awareness to see how we behave when we fail. The practices help to increase the awakening of being, in order to just be here, under all circumstances, in constant relationship with the Divine. You can go to the Gospels and the Qur'an and you'll find the words of this message in there. These words we've been repeating all of our lives are saying something quite extraordinary. They're saying Allah alone is sufficient. It's miraculous. You need nothing else. The Divine is at the beck and call of your soul, but not your fantasies, and not your ego.

It's quite extraordinary, if you re-read the sacred revelations to humanity, especially, the Qur'an. The Divine promises you everything you need. If you co-operate with it. This is not to be interpreted as, "I can attain quantum affluence by my positive thinking." You can obtain the bliss and the security of your soul by surrendering everything to that One.

> I have found the Soul of souls,
> let this soul of mine be taken.
> I've forgotten gain and loss,
> let this shop of mine be plundered.
> I've passed beyond my very self,
> I've removed the veils before me.
> I am together with the Friend,
> let these doubts of mine fall away.
> My own ego abandoned me,
> the Friend took everything I had.
> Those who give and take are friends,
> let this language of mine be jumbled.
> I cut all ties and went to the Friend,
> I fell in with God.
> Let my poems be scattered.
> I became tired of two-ness,
> and ate at the table of Oneness.
> I drank the wine of suffering,
> let all my remedies be thrown out.
> Since this journey of being began,
> the Friend has rushed to meet us.
> Light has filled the ruins of this heart,
> let this universe of mine be shattered.
> I have passed up dreams,
> I have tired of summers and winters.
> I have found the Gardener of flowers,
> let this garden of mine be dug up.
> Yunus, you say it well, smooth as honey.
> I have found the Honey of honeys,
> let this hive of mine be given away.

Sometimes, I think that nowhere else in literature is the spirit of pure dervishhood embodied as fully and beautifully as in the writing of Yunus. I say that with full awareness that we are of Mevlana's tradition, and not to detract from Mevlana's gifts. Mevlana offers us an exalted Truth, extraordinary knowledge, and a glimpse of extraordinary Love. In Yunus, I have a feeling of what it is like to be a dervish, and what it is to be inside dervishhood.

"I have found the Honey of honeys, let this hive of mine be given away." This passage tells us something profound is happening in the state Yunus is in. Everything out there—including Yunus's "hive," and everything Yunus would call his own—is secondary. It is not what's needed. Yunus is in a state of awakened I-ness. He is in Unity with the Divine. All the other stuff Yunus spent his whole life trying to get into position, arrange, build, and own doesn't matter. "I've tasted the wine of suffering, let all my remedies be thrown out." He is in Unity with the Soul of souls. "Since this journey of being began, the Friend has rushed to meet us."

The real agency here is from the Friend. We're not doing very much. We have our practices, our disciplines, and the container of our Tradition. All of this is beautiful and absolutely essential. However, the real action is coming from Elsewhere.

"My own ego abandoned me." People are so afraid of surrender. But then for some, one day the ego just leaves. It's the easy way to enlightenment. God knows how it happens, and for whom, or when. It's probably after a long period of devotion, effort, sacrifice, pain, and sorrow. But we are reminded here that the Friend has never been absent. The Friend has never *not* been arranging the details of our education.

Supplication:
Why Certain Prayers Are Not Answered

IN A STORY FROM RUMI'S *Masnavi*, there is a farmer who wanted to learn the language of the animals. He went to the Prophet Moses and asked for this gift. Moses told the man he was not ready for something like that. The farmer pleaded with Moses on several occasions. Finally, God told Moses to give the farmer what he wanted. Moses protested to God that this would destroy the farmer. God directed Moses to give the farmer just a little bit of the gift. Moses proceeded to teach the farmer the speech of the dog and the rooster. The farmer thanked Moses and ran back to his farm.

As he approached, he overheard the dog and the rooster arguing. The dog was complaining that the rooster had eaten all the breadcrumbs and had not left anything for him. The rooster told the dog not to worry because tomorrow the dog would have a feast. The dog asked how that would be. The rooster told the dog that the mule was going to die tomorrow and that he'd have plenty of meat to eat. Having heard this, the farmer hurried and sold the mule before it died. He pocketed a nice profit and escaped the disaster of having lost the mule. As a result of this good outcome, the farmer became very interested in listening to what else the rooster and dog would talk about.

The next day he eavesdropped on their conversation. He heard the dog complaining again to the rooster for having eaten all the breadcrumbs and leaving him with no food. The rooster again tells the dog not to worry because tomorrow the horse is going to die and the dog would have a big feast. The farmer heard this and once again managed to avoid the tragedy by selling the horse before it died.

Supplication: Why Certain Prayers Are Not Answered

A few days later, the farmer overheard the ox was about to die and so again he sold the animal before it died. The farmer thought that he could now avoid all disaster and thanked God for the gift of being able to understand the language of animals. And later the farmer overheard the dog and rooster talking again. This time the dog was really annoyed. The rooster told him not to worry. He told the dog he would have a huge feast soon because the farmer was going to die next and there would be plenty of food at the funeral. On hearing this, the farmer panicked. He ran to Moses for help. The farmer informed Moses that he was about to die and asked what he should do. Moses told the farmer to go sell himself.

We are reflecting on a certain kind of prayer known as supplication, or *dua*. Sometimes, as in the story about the farmer, prayers can be misguided. We are told in the Qur'an that, *As it is, human beings often pray for things that are harmful as if they were praying for that which is good: for people are inclined to be hasty.*[47]

This is elaborated in a *hadith* regarding the practice of asking something of God in prayer:

> Perhaps an answer has been delayed so that something greater will be given to the one who asked. You might have asked and not been given it, but something greater than that for which you asked was given in this world and the next, or perhaps something was withheld from you for your own good. Something that you seek may have been destructive to your *deen* had it been given. Ask for something of lasting benefit and let its affliction be removed from you. Your possessions will not remain for you nor will you remain for them.

The word *deen* is commonly translated as "religion," but we could also translate it as "life transaction." *Deen* is what we transact with eternity. *Deen* is what our lives will finally add up to and what our relationship to eternity and truth is. It is "religion" in the sense

---

47. Surah al-Isra' 17:11.

that whatever our ultimate beliefs and values are, that is our *deen*. The Qur'an says, *To you your religion, to me mine.*[48] This means everybody has their religion and there is no compulsion in the *deen*. The essence of Islamic law for all times has been that you cannot force anything upon anybody in matters of *deen*.

"Perhaps something was withheld from you for your own good. Something that you seek may have been destructive to your *deen* had it been given." How often do we really reflect on the things we want and ask for and whether receiving them would be good for our religion or destructive?

A *Hadith Qudsi* conveyed by Jafar as-Sadiq[49] says: "Whoever occupies himself with remembrance of Me instead of asking for something from Me, I will bestow something better than what I bestow on those who ask from Me."

An example of this would be choosing and holding a meaningful or sacred word or a *zhikr* in order to understand the power of the word. These teachings can help inform the practice of *zhikr* because of their language and their purpose of connecting us to the Divine. Choosing a Divine Name or any true human quality can activate that Divine Attribute within us.

But in other cases, it may seem that our supplications are not answered. Why is that? Because you call out to One whom you do not really know and you ask from One you do not understand. Need is the essence of the *deen*. "If one is blind to Allah," says Jafar as-Sadiq, "the prayer will bring disappointment because whoever is unaware of the lowliness of his ego, whoever is not aware that his heart and its innermost secrets are under Allah's power, will think he is asking of Allah in matters of request and of supplication. This is presumption before God."

It is quite extraordinary to read "whoever is not aware that his heart and its innermost secrets are under Allah's power." This refers to a deep, inner faculty of the human being for meeting and

---

48. *Surah al-Kafirun* 109:6.
49. The sixth Shia Imam and also a major figure in the Hanafi and Maliki schools of Sunni jurisprudence.

Supplication: Why Certain Prayers Are Not Answered

knowing the Divine. This faculty is directly under the power of God Himself. To supplicate at the level that Jafar as-Sadiq is trying to teach, we would have to be able to go to that very deep, silent, still part of ourselves and supplicate from there.

In our Tradition, supplication is the practice of calling on the Divine directly. We may have our hands held open and speak spontaneously, in a memorized prayer, or even in imitation of the words of some of the prophets or their companions. Having that direct dialogue with the Divine is called *dua*, and is an example of the powerful use of language.

There are various levels of *dua*. At the first and most basic level, people ask for the wellbeing of others and themselves, and for protection against calamities. Another level of understanding during supplication unfolds when people are in *tariqah*, the esoteric path. It is the level of asking for deeper awareness and awakening, beyond satisfying the demands of the body and the *nafs*. At the third level of *haqiqah* or the deepest reality, prayer and supplication are of an altogether different quality. The worship of people living at this level reflects the Divine Qualities such as Mercy and Beauty, just as the way they live is an expression of the Divine Agency in the world. These three levels exist in worship, in fasting, and in everything.

In our Tradition, we include as our teachers all of the prophets including Abraham, Moses, and Jesus, and the Prophet Muhammad, peace be upon them all. These spiritual educators are close to us. We benefit from their examples. By reflecting on their words, perhaps we glimpse how subtle, mature, and deep the education they provide is.

We are being taught that there is even an *adab* in approaching the Divine and that it is based in humility as well as a sense of our own nothingness and need.

This is what we love about Jafar as-Sadiq, Ali, and the Prophet Muhammad. They are teaching true sincerity in asking us to examine our motivations, purify ourselves of our self-assertion, and let go of our presumptions in order to be in a pure relationship with the Truth.

There are some teachings that are so utterly merciful and generous that we can only weep, as in, "I am in whatever conception my servant holds of Me." God will enter even into a limited concept or idea. This merciful teaching puts the heart at rest. It is telling us that all can be forgiven; there is no sin, mistake, or harm that we have done to our souls that Allah cannot cover with His mercy. We are given this assurance and we can go away secure in that love. Perhaps then we can hear other teachings and begin the more fastidious work. We may realize the true state of our own *nafs* and our continual self-assertion in our everyday life. We may then realize that we cannot even pray or supplicate to Allah unless we are coming from that deep core. We see what is and are humbled and even ashamed by what we see in order that, maybe for once in our lives, we can utter a true prayer, a true call, a *dua*.

The Essence of the *Hadiths*

WITH ISLAM, SOMETHING CAME INTO THE WORLD that shifted humanity and brought about a heightening of God-consciousness in people. There's no doubt about that. The freedom accompanying this heightened consciousness was the absolute center of Muhammad's message. It was not a theological message. It was not an exclusive, sectarian message; it was about a God who cannot ever be fully conceptualized, described, or limited by our thoughts or beliefs. The message was about making God the center of our reality. It emphasized and demonstrated how we depend on this Reality. All grace and goodness come from this Reality, but we are responsible, too. The message is not that we are to turn everything over to God and let Him do it all. In fact we carry a great responsibility to seek knowledge; not just information, but knowing. I think that will be made really evident in the following *hadith*.

The messenger of God, peace be upon him, said,

> If anyone travels a path in search of knowledge, God will conduct him through one of the paths of paradise. The angels will lower their wings, delighted with the one who seeks knowledge. And the inhabitants of the heavens and the earth, and the fish in the depths of the water will seek forgiveness for him. The higher station of the gnostic over the worshipper is like the position of the full moon among the stars.

The *hadith* is not talking about the sect of Gnostics, but rather the knowers of God. The knowers of God are the heirs of the Prophet. The heirs did not inherit any money. They have only inherited knowledge, and whoever attains to it is one who has abundant fortune.

Much of Muhammad's wisdom is very practical and relational. The *hadiths* connect the human to the world and everything in it. The Messenger said, "You will never be able to meet the demands of the people with your wealth, so meet them with your courtesy and manners."

The *hadiths* address many aspects of life because Muhammad cared so much about his people. His sayings stem from the love that comes out of the responsibility he took for caring for everyone: "The best and most noble kind of companionship is to maintain relations with a bad-mannered person until he improves in his behavior."

One of the themes in many of the *hadiths* is that we belong to God. We're visitors here and this is the place where we have been sent to carry out a certain type of conscious behavior and service. The type of service that is needed is spelled out quite clearly in the *hadiths*. They set a baseline for self-sacrifice, courtesy, and generosity.

The Messenger of God, peace be upon him, said,

> Purity completes faith. Praise fills the scale. Glorification and praise fill what is in between the heavens and earth. Prayer is light. Charity is evidence. Patience enlightens. And the Qur'an is an argument for you or against you. Everyone sets out each day and trades his soul, either emancipating it or oppressing it.

Consider this *hadith*: "If people knew what lies in abandonment of desires they would race toward it and if they knew what blessings lie in the prayers of the night and morning they would come to them even if they had to crawl to do so."

That *hadith* seems very unusual because it's a little extreme. It's telling us that we have a relationship with the Unseen that is of extraordinary benefit if we could see things as they are. We always see relatively. So much of what we see is based on how we are and the state we're in at that particular moment. Sometimes we look with negative eyes at something that is beautiful and miss the beauty that is there. There are times when we look at something that others think is ugly but we see only the beauty of it.

This *hadith* offers compassion for the agony of separation and the anguish of not knowing, both of which characterize us as humans. It points out that it's a very human state to not know and to be in the state of not knowing when there is a Path. This little *hadith* offers an even bigger message: not only do we typically lack a sense of the benefits of night prayers, but sometimes we're going as fast as we can in the other direction. We are usually fleeing the mystery of the night, going into separation and not giving a moment to stillness.

Mu'Adh ibn Jabal recorded that the messenger of God, peace be upon him, said, "God most exalted, said, 'My love belongs by right to those who love one another in me, to those who sit together in me, to those who visit one another in me, and to those who give generously to one another in me.'"

By saying "My love belongs" to those people, it's become a promise from God. This *hadith* highlights the importance of companionship and being friends when walking on the Path.

The *hadiths* are full of practical and down-to-earth advice. It's common sense, yet very beautiful and merciful as well.

Someone shared with me that they had set an alarm on their phone to make *adhan*, the call to prayer. She said it had been interesting to watch how her mind responded to the alarm. Typically it was with the thought, "I can't pray right now in this moment." She also shared the feeling of frustration that the call to prayer was interrupting what she was doing. She noted how five times each day she had the opportunity to see this reaction and then remember, "Who does the time really belong to?" Even though the experience of prayer was a good one, that feeling of being interrupted went on and on. This type of experience can provide a way to understand why one of God's names could be "the Interrupter."

The *hadiths* provide the knowledge of how to live in the human state. We see there is a possibility of peace, acceptance, trust, courage, and love, and all that is from contact with this transcendent Reality. This is the answer to the incompleteness inherent in our spiritual longing. The machinations of our ego, the search for satisfactions for our body and our self, can be transformed and brought into a state of harmony. The Prophet showed us how to do this. He embodied the message and provided the knowledge we need to practice that. In this way, Muhammad passed on some knowledge about how to deal with our own incompleteness and unknowing.

One *hadith* shows there is an element of divine, conscious deliberation when facing options. The *hadith's* suggestion is for us to more and more often frame the dilemmas and needs of our life in a perspective that is bigger than our typical narrow perspective of "I want this" and "I want it like this, not like that." Here is that *hadith*:

> The messenger of God, peace be upon him, said, "When one of you is uncertain about what you should do in a particular situation, pray two extra cycles of the ritual prayer, then offer the following prayer, known as the *istikhara* prayer: 'Oh God, I ask You of Your knowledge for guidance and of Your power for strength. And I ask You of Your great abundance. Certainly You are powerful and I am not. And you are the Knower of the unknown. O God, if You know this matter [*here the supplicant should substitute for the words "this matter" whatever it is specifically that he has in mind, for example this "journey," or "marriage," etc.*] to be good for my religion, my worldly life, my life in the next world, my present state of affairs or my future state, then ordain it for me, make it easy for me, and bless me in it. But if You know this matter to be harmful to my religion, my worldly life, my life in the next world, my present state of affairs or my future state, turn it away from me and turn me away from it. Ordain good for me wherever it may be and then make me content with it.'"

The *hadiths* convey the sweetness, mercy, and humility that are the basis for Muslims saying, "If you want to be a Muslim, model yourself on Muhammad. He is the perfected human being. He's not a son of God or a saint. He's a real human being. This state is attainable."

This *hadith*, for instance, "The most intelligent person is the one who is most fastidious in courtesy and friendship," is telling us to be more scrupulous with ourselves. The *hadith* is saying to be fastidious about our own courtesy and friendships. It's not about our expectations. It's not about looking outside of ourselves. It's about looking within ourselves.

Some of the *hadiths* have messages about knowledge. We are told very personal aspects about knowledge and pursuing knowledge. Matters like courtesy and friendship may at first seem like they are unrelated. But in a way, cultivating fastidiousness in these matters is an example of how to keep the mirror of your heart polished so that you do not let a counterfeit, know-it-all kind of knowledge stand in the way of true knowledge. Everything in the *hadiths* protects us from the obstructions of the ego.

The Arabic word for knowledge, *'ilm*, is one of the most frequently appearing nouns in the Qur'an. This indicates its importance. In virtually all cases in which knowledge is talked about in the Qur'an, it's talked about as something that is given by the Divine. It's not something that is necessarily given in books. It is not imposed on you by authority. Knowledge is given to a human being. The human being has a great capacity for reflection. There is, however, one kind of knowledge that can be a veil and the result of opinion, prejudice, and preconceptions; and another kind of knowledge that arises within as a gift, a grace.

This higher knowledge begins with a type of "not knowing," the humility to ask for guidance. There are a number of *hadiths* that make the necessity of asking for knowledge very clear. Knowledge comes after it's asked for. This is such a humble plea, and it's coming from the Prophet. "Show me what to do, God, and make me want to do that." Ibn Arabi, the great thirteenth-century Sufi, begins his essay on "What the Seeker Needs" by saying, "May we learn to know and love what you, God, love for us."

There are a number of places in the Qur'an where it says, "These are signs, could they not use their intelligence?" This signifies we have something innate that can draw us closer to Reality.

Someone might ask, "Is this innate quality the heart or some other faculty?" I would answer that we have the heart, and we have intelligence. The word for this in the Qur'an is *'aql*. It refers to our reasoning as well as to our intelligence. Reason derives principles from our experience. The heart provides another kind of knowledge: intuition and a subtle qualitative way of knowing. The human being has many subtle faculties of knowing, but it's important as well to include reason and common sense. I once asked Celalettin Celebi Efendi, the head of the Mevlevi tradition at the time, whether we should follow our heart or our reason. He said, "It's best when they both agree."

The Prophet's Character: What the *Hadiths* Really Say

IT WAS A ROUGH AND RAW TIME in many ways when the Prophet lived. It was the seventh century A.D. Most of the world was in the Dark Ages. Arabia was a backwater. There wasn't much there: a few tribal societies in the middle of the desert. Yet as Islam emerged from the Arabian peninsula, it became a transforming power unprecedented in history. It was an extraordinary explosion of knowledge, study, science, and arts from a small group of Arabs who learned about Islam from the life of a man who was illiterate.

Within a few years of the Prophet's death, there were people traveling all over the face of the earth collecting and sharing his sayings, known as the *hadiths*. Without the example of his character embodied in the *hadiths*, the civilization, culture, and learning of Islam as a transformative societal force would not have emerged. The values expressed in the *hadiths* are central to the message of the Messenger's own life. I'll share with you some real stories that illustrate this.

The blessed Ali was the son-in-law of the Prophet and one of his closest companions. He was to be the fourth caliph after Muhammad. Someone had a dream or a vision that a certain person was going to assassinate Ali. The one receiving this message found the man who was the assassin in the dream and told him what he was going to do. When the man heard this, he said, "God forbid, if that is to be true." The man went to Ali and said "Kill me now. Don't let me do this." Ali said, "If I were to kill you now it would be unjust. You haven't committed any crime."

But later, the man did indeed stab Ali. As Ali was dying, some people brought him a glass of milk. Ali said, "Take it to the man who stabbed me." The people did as Ali had said and brought the milk to the man. They said to him, "Ali sent this milk." The man was in such a darkened state he wouldn't take it and said, "It must be poisoned." This story illustrates that there really were people who were living in the way set out in the *hadiths*. Ali was one of them.

A man once asked the Prophet Muhammad to tell him about nobility of character. He said, "It means that you should forgive him who has wronged you, re-establish ties with him who has broken them off, give to him who has denied you something, and speak the truth even if it is against your own interests." In talking about nobility of character, the *hadith* says to "forgive him who has wronged you." That forgiveness is a sign of a noble character. The message is about raising your character to be above the common level. The words, "re-establish ties with him who has broken them off" is encouraging us to overcome our own ego. It requires humility and freedom from your own ego as well.

"Join with him who cuts you off, give to him who withholds from you." This magnanimous impulse lived on among the inheritors of the Prophet. Seven centuries after Ali there was a man who had vehemently criticized Ibn Arabi. When that man died, Ibn Arabi started fasting. After weeks of fasting, somebody asked Ibn Arabi, "Why are you fasting?" He replied, "I will fast until Allah forgives this man for what he said about me." Weeks passed. One day Ibn Arabi smiled, started to eat, and said, "Allah has forgiven him." That's a story about living in both worlds and doing good in both worlds.

There is a similar call to nobility by the *hadith* "Give to him who has denied you something." The word for the Divine Attribute of nobility is *al-Kareem*, which we also translate as "the Generous." Among the pre-Islamic Arabs, nobility was associated with generosity. Generosity means that you give your best. You don't hold back. Nobility and generosity are intimately related in this word *kareem*. There's a beautiful saying in the Qur'an which we translate as, *We have ennobled the children of Adam.*[50] Another way

---

50. Surah al-Isra' 17:70.

to translate it is, *We have given this noble nature to all human beings*, and *We have honored the human being*. A human can be both noble and generous. That is the honor and nobility of the human being.

This conviction about the nobility of the human being is at the core of the prophetic tradition going back to Abraham, through Jesus and all the prophets. Humans occupy a privileged place within creation. This has been sometimes misunderstood to mean humans have the privilege of exploiting the Earth. The Qur'an addresses this misunderstanding in passages that warn against spreading corruption and injustice upon the earth. Our station as noble beings has to be lived out as the *hadith* suggests.

Imagine the kind of society such striving would create. Contrast that with what we often see in the news, what our politicians do and how they treat each other. Political candidates show a total lack of respect for each other as human beings. Imagine if people were to begin to live in the way the *hadiths* suggest we live. It might begin as a small community, a subculture, but eventually grow into a society that lived with respect for other human beings. I maintain that this is how early Islam spread so quickly and widely; this is how a great civilization was created.

The prayer the Prophet Muhammad would recite when he approached a village for the first time conveys a sense that whenever the Prophet did anything there was a beautiful sense of mindfulness. He would say, "O Allah, I ask You for the good of this place and the good You have gathered within it. I seek refuge in You from the evil of it, and the evil You have gathered in it. O Allah, sustain us through those who live here and protect us from harm in this place, and make the inhabitants to love us as You make us to love the righteous ones among them." Every moment he was turning towards that transcendent Reality. His prayer extends goodness and blessings to all beings. The ending of the prayer is both a connection to everyone there and to the One. This *hadith* leaves us with a feeling that it was customary and conventional to give minute-by-minute blessings in life and to be in deep connection in the most ordinary moments. It has a mirroring and reciprocal effect. It is a prayer that the people of the town will respond in love to him as God responds to the holy people in that town. The prayer is to amplify what's already there. It's offering the best of that community.

Some of the people of Mecca were very skeptical about the revelation of the Qur'an and of the prophetic role of Muhammad. They complained, "Why didn't God send an angel? Why did he send an ordinary person?" Soon thereafter there were some verses in the Qur'an that were revealed to the Prophet in which the Divine said, *We sent one from among yourselves and gave the message to one from among yourselves.*[51] In other words, He sent a person, not as the message but as an embodiment of the message.

While embodying Divine inspiration, the *hadiths* also bring us down to earth in a very practical way. The Prophet, peace and blessings upon him, said, "If two Muslims meet, then be the most beloved of them in the eyes of God and the best of them by your more joyful encounter with your companion. When two Muslims shake hands, God makes 100 mercies descend upon them, 90 of them being for the one who began the handshake." To have a joyful countenance, the Prophet said, is a form of charity. It's a giving to others. A smile may be the best charity you can give. Our happiness should testify to our being in remembrance.

---

51. Surah al-Jumu'ah 62:2.

The Prophet on the Perfection of Character

THERE ARE MANY SUFI LINEAGES. These are called "orders". Some of them are Sunni, others are Shia. But to tell you the truth, Sufis do not make too much of the differences among the orders. Even though the different lineages have different styles and temperaments, there are things that unite the Sufi lineages. What makes for an extraordinary and beautiful sense of connection is that we have a common vocabulary. We have a common spiritual practice, namely the five daily prayers of Islam. We have the Qur'an. As a result, there is an amazing coherence among our communities. Sufis from all over the world could all come together, as they often do, and immediately be on the same page. There is communication, and no fundamental arguments about the nature of things, even if each comes from such different parts of the world as Bosnia, Indonesia, or Pakistan.

There is no external authority in Sufism. There is no leader like a pope or a head Sufi. There is, however, an inner coherence. The single most beautiful coherence that unites all the Sufi lineages is our love of the Prophet Muhammad. But we can't love Muhammad if we don't know Muhammad.

Shams of Tabriz said:

> We owe so much to the Prophet Muhammad who opened up a way when there wasn't one. He rode his horse through all these obstacles and opened up the path for us. He's the kind of man before whom even angels lay down their ladders. Even acrobats who astound people on a high wire with amazing feats are amazed at the length and the strength of Muhammad's rope. Anyone who has ever seen Prophet Muhammad riding upon a huge black lion and cropping it as if it were a lazy donkey can only fall down in admiration of him.

Rumi himself wrote in his *Discourses* (*Fihi ma Fihi*), in the discourse entitled "Manifest Signs," about the singularity of the Prophet Muhammad:

> It's strange for you to have a state in which there is no room for Muhammad when Muhammad has no state in which there is no room for a creature like you. After all, the state you have attained is because of him and through his influence. All gifts are first showered upon him. Only then are they distributed through him to others. Such is the custom. God said, "Peace be with you, O Prophet, and God's mercy. We shower you with all gifts." The Prophet added: "*And* upon God's righteous servants."
>
> God's way was extremely terrifying and blocked by snow. Since the Prophet risked his life first to drive his horse forward in order to clear the way, whoever goes this way does so because of his guidance and favor. He first discovered the way, leaving signposts everywhere to say, "Do not go this way!" "Do not go that way!" and "If you go that way, you will perish like the people of Ad and Thamud," and "If you go this way, you will find salvation like the faithful."
>
> The whole Qur'an expresses this one thing: "Therein are manifest signs" [3:97]. That is, we have put signposts along these routes. If anyone intends to tear down any of these posts, everyone will set upon him and say, "Why are you ruining our route? Are you trying to get us killed? Are you a highwayman?" Now realize that the leader is Muhammad. Until one reaches Muhammad, one does not reach us.

Now I wanted to share a page of quotes from the Prophet Muhammad to give us a taste of that love shared by Mevlana and Shams. This is a practical side of Sufism. A lot of these quotes are about the ethical, interpersonal dimension of life. These are sayings I particularly love and find most meaningful and useful.

The Messenger of God, peace be upon him, said, "God helps a man as long as he helps his brother. If anyone pursues a separate path in search of knowledge, God will thereby make easy for him a path to Paradise. Any group that gathers in one of the Houses of God to recite God's Book and study it together will have stillness descend upon them and mercy from God, and the angels surround them and God will mention them from among those near to Him. And anyone who shirks his spiritual practice will receive no special privilege through his lineage."

This is a bit of a description of why Sufis gather in groups and the importance of being together. One of our teachers said, "One log in a fireplace will not burn very well, but if you stack up a few logs, with a little kindling, you can get a good fire going." In so many ways, we need each other, energetically, to learn from each other's qualities and to be inspired by each other's commitment.

In the sentence, "If anyone pursues a separate path in search of knowledge…" the knowledge we're talking about is spiritual knowledge and knowledge of the Real. It is knowledge of what is going to matter to our souls and our lives. "God will also make easy for him or her a path to paradise." The word for paradise is actually "garden" or *jannah* in Arabic. Paradise is not just something that comes after this earthly life. The Qur'an says, *The Garden will be brought near to all those who are in a state of God-consciousness.*[52] To all those who deepen in their remembrance, deepen in presence, *The Garden will be brought near.*

For us it's not two worlds. The two worlds are simultaneous and inter-penetrating. It's not that we don't consider where we will be after we leave this physical body. But here and now, heaven and earth, also have the potential to combine.

The Messenger of God, peace be upon him, said, "You will never be able to meet the demands of the people with your wealth, so meet them with your courtesy and manners."

It's hard to imagine a more practical, beneficial principle for a mother or father to teach their daughter or son. The importance of manners in the life of the Prophet was extraordinary. He said, "I have

---

52. *Surah ash-Shu'ara* 26:90.

been sent to this world to perfect character." Character is the ripened fruit of spiritual consciousness. We're not seeking spiritual consciousness to have extraordinary states of experience. It is rather that experiences of a spiritual nature, of a higher consciousness, will inevitably affect character and bring an awareness of how we respect each other, the courtesy we extend, and our friendliness. All of these reflect on, purify, and develop the soul.

Another *hadith* says, "The most intelligent of people are those most fastidious in matters of courtesy and friendship."

These are the principles, and hundreds more like them, that have shaped the Sufi brotherhoods and sisterhoods. There's a teaching in our Tradition that if anyone has hurt our feelings, we are obliged to go to them, privately, within three days, and communicate to them about the pain we've experienced, in order to attempt to set it right. We have three days in which to either resolve the situation or drop it. It's a religious obligation. Likewise, any kind of backbiting, gossip, or slander is considered a very grievous sin. They asked the Prophet Muhammad, "What if what we're saying about that person is true?" He said, "That's what I mean by backbiting. If it's not true, it's also a lie and slander." They asked, "What do you mean?" He said, "Backbiting is saying anything behind somebody's back which if they heard you repeating or saying would hurt them."

This is how we keep the atmosphere clean on all levels. There is no inner and outer. We're responsible for every thought. Thought is action. Thought has its effect in the spiritual and psychic world. Every negative thought is felt consciously, or at least unconsciously, by others. To be pure-hearted is to be continually cleaning ourselves of these kinds of judgments.

The Messenger of God, peace be upon him, said to some of his companions, "Why is it that I do not see the sweetness in your worship?" When they asked him what "sweetness in worship" was, he replied, "Humility."

Worship is one of the essentials. It's why, in our Tradition, prayer is supposed to be five times a day, at appointed times. But what is worship? Worship can be in the company of others, in a mosque, or it can be done alone. Worship is taking time from the momentum of our lives to stop and stand before the Face of God for a few minutes. The prostrations in the ritual prayer that are the regular practice of the Islamic tradition, and which Sufis also do, include four to eight cycles of standing, bowing, and prostrating. At most, the ritual prayer takes between five and ten minutes. It's a deep and mindful encounter with the Infinite Face of God, not performing a ritual with rote recitations. In fact, the Prophet Muhammad, peace be upon him, said, "If your ritual prayer is not done with presence, it's not worship." Presence is absolutely essential to the ritual prayer. The whole normative practice of Islam, its basic practices and rituals, are a spiritual training system when properly understood.

People worshipping and praying at regular intervals during each day is one of the beautiful things about visiting a country like Turkey and regions where these practices are still maintained, like in Konya. All people, even shopkeepers, take a break from their activities at mid-day, mid-afternoon, sunset, and just after sunset. They may walk off to a mosque, which is never more than a five-minute walk in these traditional cities, or they may worship and pray in a back room of their shops. They dive into the Divine Ocean for a few minutes and then they come back, refreshed and with a whole different energy. This is very real and very practical.

These are techniques of awakening intentionality, greater awareness, a relationship, and an encounter with the Divine. Week after week, year after year these deepen. One of our friends, a great Sufi teacher, recently said, "Everything is in the prostration." When our foreheads touch the ground we enter into that Divine Oblivion. It is oblivion, in the sense that we are so present with the Divine that everything else just disappears. We're completely there in the consciousness of the Divine, forehead to the ground, for that moment. It's a kind of bliss.

Earlier, I talked about expanding presence and that our presence goes beyond the boundaries of our bodies. We're not just a result of a little electrical impulse somewhere in a brain or something with a heart pumping blood through our bodies. What we are extends far beyond that. Scientifically, it's been proven that our thoughts can be felt on the other side of the continent, if we're coherent enough.

We are much more than this package of flesh and bone. Even more importantly, while our presence is expansive, we're in the Divine Presence. How could we not be conscious of it?

We cannot recount too often the beautiful *hadith* from Muadh ibn Jabal, who reported that the Messenger of God, peace be upon him, said, "God, Most Exalted, has said, 'My Love by right belongs to those who love one another in Me, to those who sit together in Me, to those who visit one another in Me, and to those who give generously to one another in Me.'"

As we sit here together, we're here to be together in that state of presence. My function is just to remind each of you of it. What we hear serves to remind us of these truths, as well as how to make this real and bring our own certitude to this group consciousness. We're not allowed to say or describe anything we haven't personally experienced or know as reality. We are not asked to believe anything but our own experiences.

Abu Dharr asked the Messenger of God, peace be upon him, whether he had seen His Lord. He replied, "He is Light, where shall I see Him? He is the Light by which I see."

The Qur'an says, *God is the Light of the heavens and the earth.*[53] In other words, God is the Light of the Unseen world and the visible world. The Divine Reality is that through which perception exists. Saint Francis and other saints have said, "The one you're searching for is the one looking through your eyes."

Abu Hurairah related that when a desert Arab got up and urinated in the mosque, the people seized him, but the Prophet, peace be upon him, said to them, "Leave him alone and pour a bucket of water over what he has passed, for you have been sent only to make things easy, not to make things difficult."

---

53. Surah an-Nur (24:35).

In another instance, the Prophet said, "Woe to anyone who makes religion difficult for others."

Maybe now we have a sense of why the Prophet Muhammad is beloved to us, why his character has inspired the Sufis, and how this has helped to create communities, brotherhoods, and sisterhoods in which a beautiful quality of affection and mutual respect became the norm.

Some Sayings of Hazrati Ali

WE NEED THE INSPIRATION of beings like the Prophet Muhammad, Rumi, and Hazrati Imam Ali, and others who spoke to us the way they have.

Ali was the son-in-law and one of the closest companions of the Prophet Muhammad, as well as a key link in the chain of transmission of Sufism. It's through him that this hidden, living Tradition of mysticism has come down from the time of the Prophet through the generations to Rumi and other great Sufis, and then eventually into the present.

Ali's wisdom emerged within the context of Muhammad's message in the Qur'an and continued its flow into the teachings of Shams of Tabriz and into Rumi. Shams is the one who transformed Rumi from Jalaluddin into Mevlana ("our Master") Jalaluddin Rumi.

There are many extraordinary things about Ali, who is also known as Imam Ali. He was one of the greatest Arabic orators. Through his gift of language, Ali could convey much with few words. Ali was also one of the greatest calligraphers and swordsmen. He often demonstrated extraordinary courage.

His sayings are filled with very practical advice. It's the sort of advice we could give to our children, keep for ourselves, and share with people from all walks of life. The sayings are not dependent upon a belief system. They are based on truth. Here is some of Ali's advice:

The word of God is the medicine of the heart.

Lead such a life that when you die the people may mourn you, and while you are alive they long for your company.

Generosity hides shortcomings.

A man's behavior is the index of his mind.

A man who praises himself displays his deficiency of intellect.

The tongue of a wise man lies behind his heart.

A wise enemy is better than a foolish friend.

Silence is the best reply to a fool.

Speech is like a medicine, a small dose of which cures, but an excess of which kills.

As a man's wisdom increases, so his desire to speak decreases.

Finding fault in others is one's greatest fault.

Haste is a species of madness.

Greed is perpetual enslavement.

Knowledge is the ornament of the rich, and the riches of the poor.

He who teaches you even one letter binds you with a fetter of gratitude.

Truth is bitter, but its result is sweet; falsehood appears to be sweet, but it is poisonous in its effect.

He who does not know should not be ashamed to learn.

Do not run after the world; let the world run after you.

He who is aware of his own faults is oblivious to the faults of others.

Contentment is the treasure which is never exhausted.

No relationship is stronger than the relationship that exists between man and God.

Whatever harm accrues of silence can be remedied, but whatever harm is done because of speech cannot be remedied.

It is better to restrain your desires than to stretch your hand before others.

A little that is earned because of honest labor is better than a larger amount gained through dishonest means.

Mevlana had tremendous respect and appreciation for Ali, as several passages from *Discourses of Rumi (Fihi ma Fihi)* illustrate. Discourse 7, entitled "The Resurrection is Now," makes clear that the truth conveyed by the Prophet Muhammad and Hazrati Ali is a truth for all humanity:

> In this world everyone is preoccupied with something. Some are preoccupied with love for women, others with possessions, and still others with making money and some with learning. Each one believes that his wellbeing and happiness depend upon that preoccupation. That also is God's mercy. When a man goes after it in search and does not find it, he turns his back on it. After pausing a while he says: "That joy and mercy must be sought. Maybe I did not look enough. Let me search again." When he seeks again he still does not find it, but he continues until the mercy manifests itself unveiled. Only then does he realize that he was on the wrong track before.
>
> God however has some servants who see clearly even before the resurrection. Ali said, "If that veil were lifted, I would not be more certain." By this he meant that if the shell of appearances was taken away and the Day of Reckoning was to come, his certitude would not increase. His perception was like a group of people who go into a dark room at night and pray, each facing a different direction. When day breaks, they all turn around. All except the one man who had been facing Mecca all night long. Since the

others now turned to face his direction why should he turn around? Those servants of God face him even during the night. They have turned away from all that is other than Him. For them, the resurrection is immediate and present.

[*Fihi ma Fihi*, Discourse 7]

In this passage, Rumi explains how there are people who go down the wrong path and eventually, almost by happenstance, find the right path. Rumi describes God's mercy to the people who were praying in the dark and facing the wrong direction. That said, there was one who didn't have to turn because he was already facing Mecca. That one was like Imam Ali.

There is also another story about Ali referenced in this passage. They once asked Ali: "When is the resurrection going to be?" And he answered, "You ask about the resurrection from the resurrection?"

In our Tradition, all human beings who have lived will, in some sense, be resurrected. All our deeds and actions will come to fruition and we will be resurrected in the form of our most beautiful actions. Ali is saying, "If all the veils were lifted right now I would be no more certain of this reality than I am already."

The Divine Reality has attributes of Mercy, Beauty, and Stringency. Some might call it "Wrath," rather than "Stringency." But even Wrath is really Mercy with a thin coating of Stringency. This Mercy is characteristic of the Prophet Muhammad and of Ali. It is at the heart of this whole Tradition. The revelation itself was about this Mercy. The bottom line is that it's all Mercy. Even our going astray becomes, in the end, a means to our finding our way. We may suffer by going astray, and that's a mercy too. That is a corrective.

It's all the action of Divine Intelligence, the Divine Guidance fulfilling its purpose. Its purpose is not to punish or threaten, but rather to reveal its beauty. Ali manifested such beauty in his calligraphy, speech, behavior, and ethics.

A story from the *Masnavi* provides a sense of this beauty of Ali's character, and thus of the essence of a real human being:

In the early days of Islam, the community had been driven into exile. The small group of believers had lost everything, yet was still being attacked. Permission was finally given to defend the community.

Ali was in the front lines during a battle at this time. He was just about to deliver the *coup de grace* to his opponent, when the young man spat in his face. Ali threw down his sword. His opponent asked, "Why didn't you kill me? You could have killed me just then." Ali said, "When you spat in my face you made me angry. I am not allowed to wield this sword in anger. I wield it only for the sake of justice and truth. It would have been unlawful for me to kill you in that state."

In that moment, Ali's beautiful state was reflected in the heart of this young man, who himself entered the state of surrender and became a Muslim. This is the story that Rumi chooses to end Book I of the *Masnavi*.

Be Gold Yourself, the Seven Levels of Reality

THERE ARE TWO DIFFERENT ASPECTS of Sufi practice: meditation and remembrance. We make a distinction between these two very similar and yet distinct processes. Meditation is an act of self-awareness. It's listening within, coming into your own deepest centre in order to move from the false self to what we call the essential self or higher self, the source of consciousness. Meditation is mastery of attention and observation. It is being able to observe the contents of our mind—our thoughts as well as our emotions.

Remembrance goes a step beyond meditation. Remembrance fosters an awareness and capacity that is capable of developing a relationship and a resonance with the Divine Attributes. The Divine Attributes themselves are not just aspects of the Divine. They are completely and wholly the Divine Itself. You cannot take the Divine Light and say that it is separate from the Power of the Divine, or the Love of the Divine, or the Forgiveness of the Divine. Each Divine Name is complete even while being an aspect of the Divine. Remembrance is a sense of relationship in which the individual self comes into resonance with the Divine Presence and is transformed by it.

One essential dimension of remembrance, or *zhikr*, is qualifying the breath with the Names of God. The breath touches all dimensions in a human being and through it we can experience the seven levels of Reality. The seven levels are:

1. A trust in God as our foundation and, with that trust, knowing no fear.
2. Nurturing the sensory side of our being, loving it, keeping it within the context of the Divine Reality, and

mastering it so we can be at home in this body, in this natural world.
3. Having a healthy sense of life purpose that is in service.
4. Using the heart's capacity for unconditional love and openly embracing life, relationship, the imperfect, and the unlovable.
5. Expressing that capacity creatively, appropriately, in relationship and in devotion.
6. A sense of vision connecting us to everything beyond time and space—a very refined, vibrational knowing where we perceive meanings, envision possibilities, and glimpse our sense of Unity, even beyond unconditional love.

The seventh level is virtually inexpressible. Like the Fount of Abundance, it flows upward and outward to Infinity, into the Higher Dimensionality of which we are part.

There is a poem by Hafez that encompasses all seven levels of this Reality.

You who are not yet aware, become the possessor of awareness.
If you haven't travelled, how can you be a guide?

In the Academy of Realization, pay attention to the adept of love,
so that one day, O son, you may become a father.

Wash your hands of the cheap metals of existence like the mature,
so that you may find the philosopher's stone of love and be gold
    yourself.

Sleeping and eating has kept you far away from your true level.
You will come to yourself when you give up sleeping and eating.

If the light of the love of truth falls on your heart and soul,
you will be more beautiful than the sun of the skies.

For one moment drown yourself in the sea of God, don't think
the seven seas will wet a single hair of yours.

Be Gold Yourself, the Seven Levels of Reality

From head to toe you will become the light of God
when you lose yourself on his resplendent road.

Once God's face becomes the only thing you see,
you will surely become a master of vision.

When the basis of your existence is overthrown,
empty your heart, for you will also be overthrown.

O Hafez, if your head is set on the climax of union,
be the dust on the threshold of those who can see.

The experience and process that is being talked about in this poem is something quite extraordinary. It might be that someone could read this and have no bearings and not find meaning, but someone who perhaps has travelled a certain road far enough, long enough, will have experiences to associate with the lines of this poem. A poem like this covers a whole spiritual teaching. It's all here.

"You who are not yet aware, become the possessor of awareness." Hafez is saying, *you who are not yet aware, get some awareness*. "If you haven't travelled, how can you be a guide?"

"In the Academy of Realization…" whatever that Academy may be? It's not on this Earth, it doesn't have a government endowment, it doesn't have a physical location.

"In the Academy of Realization, pay attention to the adept of love." Pay attention to what? To one who is a master of Love. To one who is matured in Love. Why? "So that one day, O son, you may become a father." The child may become a parent. Sufis are sometimes called *Ibn al-Waqt*, the "child of the moment." They live in the present moment. That is one aspect of it. To be able to live in the present. To be able to be spontaneous. Be relatively unconditioned. To be aware. Not to be tied down by the wrong kind of self-consciousness. To not hold back out of self-consciousness or fear. To be fully present in the moment.

The one who matures in that state becomes the parent. Not just the child, but the father, the mother of the moment. The one whose present moment expands. The Native Americans know this well. Their awareness, their responsibility extends to seven generations. The awareness, the present moment of that mature one goes beyond that narrow, little slice of the so called "present."

We are part of a living Tradition that has an extraordinary history for us to learn from. A glance to this past is really important because knowledge from this beautiful, living Tradition can be assimilated into our experience of the present. This assimilation merges the Tradition's history with the moment we are in and the reality we are part of. The Sufi is the son or daughter of the moment and also the parent, father or mother of the moment.

What Hafez and Mevlana Jalaluddin Rumi and every Sufi is talking about is transformation, something that is a possibility for the human being. This is very different from what people have typically made of religion. When real religion degenerates it becomes a collection of rules, a preoccupation with outer things and behavior, "correct" beliefs as opposed to incorrect beliefs.

But Sufis are concerned with Truth. *Haqq*. What is *Haqq*? What is Truth for the human being? It means *What Is Most Real*. Truth is our experience of the Divine Presence. The experience of *What Is Truly Real*. This experience is something our hearts are capable of with awareness, with consciousness. It is as if we have a sense in us, almost like a sense of sight, or smell, or touch. It is a sense of Unity, which, when it's operating, is extraordinary. We may experience it, perhaps, once in many years, as a beautiful sunset experienced when we get ourselves out of the rut of our lives, some place far away, slowed down, quiet. Suddenly we're touched by something that is not of this material world. The same sunset, which you wouldn't even notice one day, becomes a radiant experience in another moment to the heart that's open.

That opening, that receptivity, is the work of transformation. Sufis have never forgotten this. They lived this. Hafez would not be the poet he is, if he hadn't lived this process of transformation through Love.

It's not love that wants to possess or falls in love with a person. Mevlana says it's the Love that has no object. It's the Love that simply radiates Itself from the heart of the awakened human being, which is your heart, when you're awake deeply enough, when you have washed your hands of the cheap metals of existence. It's a good image. Ablution. Wash your hands once and for all of trivialities, of cheap imitations, of what is false and unreal, so that you may find the philosopher's stone of Love.

In alchemy, when you're in possession of the philosopher's stone you can make lead into gold. The philosopher's stone allows the coarser material to become refined and transformed. A teacher of ours said, "You need a little gold, to make more gold." Another teacher said, "You can have a whole ocean of milk, but if you don't have some yoghurt culture, it's never going to become yoghurt." That culture is something very small, something almost hidden, that's absolutely essential for the transformation to happen.

There are experiences the human being is potentially capable of. For the mystic, the Sufi, the lover of Truth, that experience is cultivated like yogurt or refined like gold. When consciously activated, that experience becomes more of a sustainable state of being. But how?

We go back to those simple, very reliable practices. Meditation. Remembrance. Why do these meditations work? It helps us to step back from the more superficial, mechanical parts of our thinking mind. If you're an engineer, you need to be able to think clearly and use your mind rigorously. But you won't apprehend Divine Presence through the calculations or the logic of an engineer.

With meditation, we quiet the noise, the noise that is both mental and emotional. When you allow that to quiet down enough, then you can see what *is*.

> Once God's face becomes the only thing you see,
> you will surely become a master of vision.

Hafez, having memorized the Qur'an, was well aware of the Qur'anic verse, *Wheresoever you look is the Face of God.*[54]

"Once God's face becomes the only thing you see…" you're not just looking at your thoughts, your desires, your emotional reactions, the trivialities of your contradictory desires and emotions. You've cleared some of that away. Behind that is Divine Presence, Divine Reality… a sense of order, meaningfulness, purposefulness in life. The more you give that up, the more you don't let yourself be imprisoned in the thought processes of complaining, judging, resenting, desiring, and wishing. The more you don't do that, the more that's not the primary focus of your inner life, the more you can see that your life has had purpose, that even your suffering has had purpose. More synchronicities will reveal themselves. Fortuitous accidents will prevail. Everyday life will become something quite extraordinary.

"For one moment drown yourself in the Sea of God…" People who are first getting acquainted with the idea of surrender, when they hear, "You've got to surrender, you've got to drown, you've got to 'die before you die,'" it seems terrifying. But, actually, everything preceding that is what is really terrifying. To try to be in control of the ego is terrifying. Drown yourself in the sea of God, don't think the seven seas will wet a single hair of yours. That Sea is not what it appears to be.

> From head to toe you will become the light of God,
> when you lose yourself on His resplendent road.

That's the transformation. You will become the light of God, which you always were anyway. Your consciousness, your intelligence, your very being, is like a fountain flowing from a deep inner spring that is the Divine Source.

"When the basis of your existence is overthrown…" Again, this sounds scary, to overthrow the basis of your existence which you've worked so hard to build, defend, and protect. Yet the

---

54. *Surah al-Baqarah* 2:115.

reality is that you've been using every ounce of your strength to sustain and prop up something unreal. The Qur'an is absolutely true when it says, *La hawla wa la quwwata illa billahil alliyyil azeem. There is no Power nor Agency except with God.*

Haji Bektash says, "If you want to address God, say, 'I cannot endure one moment without You!'" That's the realization of someone who knows what a waste of time our own daydreams are when compared to living in that impulse of energy and intelligence that is sourced in Infinite Energy and Intelligence, and to trusting It.

The state of being in God's presence is not something supernatural, weird, or visionary, such as seeing auras, being able to read minds, or to see the future. It's just an extraordinary sense of wellbeing, as if you were in touch with something beyond all circumstances, something that couldn't be disturbed. It's living in a continual undertone of Love. It is not the love of attraction, or possession, but the Love that has no object. It is a Love that is simultaneously love of the other and of oneself.

O Hafez, if your head is set on the climax of union,
be the dust on the threshold of those who can see.

Or as Mevlana says, "I am the dust on the threshold of Muhammad."

Thank you Hafez…

How the False Self Dissolves

IN SUFISM, we speak of stages of the *nafs* (also known as stations or *maqams*), which concern the shedding of the layers of the false self. There are three stages of *fana*, which explain the approach toward union with the Divine. The stages are *fana fi sifat*, *fana fi afal* and *fana fi dhat*.

Fana is when the unreal dissolves in the real. The false self dissolves in the being of God. The sense of separate attributes in us is annihilated. We realize our attributes or qualities are truly not our own. We experience love, patience, forgiveness, strength, and generosity and realize, "This is not me; it's a gift."

Our understanding of this may get confused as we puzzle over what this realization means. If all of our states are God's, are feelings of resentment, judgment, and blame God's as well? No. The attributes of ourselves that are separative, selfish, or negative belong to the *nafs*. That is what has to be annihilated. All such attributes must be annihilated to experience the attributes or the qualities that truly are God's. Somehow, we have to transform the negativity. There are psychological principles to be aware of here. "Transform" doesn't mean to "stuff" or "repress" the negative. The first step may be seeing what is separative, selfish, or negative. That's a big thing. Make the effort to observe, watch, and catch these attributes when they emerge in our lives. Eventually, through worship, the love of friends, wisdom, and grace, the power of that negativity, separativeness, and selfishness diminishes. There may be moments where we have an experience of irrational, unexplainable forgiveness. We've stopped blaming or resenting for a moment. Something else is coming through. It is a moment of generosity and patience. This is stage one.

The second stage, *fana fi afal*, is where we realize that our actions are not our own. In this state, we may watch ourselves

How the False self Dissolves

doing something and realize, "I could not have done that. My normal 'I' could not have done that." Such a state is exemplified in a Qur'anic *ayat* that says: *Thou didst not throw when thou threwest.*[55] This verse relates to a situation where Muhammad turned back an army that was attacking the Muslims by throwing a handful of sand at them. It was just a fistful of earth, yet the entire army was routed. *Thou didst not throw when thou threwest* refers to the fact that it was God's agency at work, not Muhammad's.

In another story, we are told the Prophet Abraham hit the sand with a staff and a spring gushed forth. It took the striking of the sand with the staff for the Divine to create the spring. The gesture alone could not have created the spring. The Divine created the flowing stream.

There are moments where we are free of self, allowing a greater power to come into the world through us to orchestrate our actions and their outcomes. The account from the Qur'an was an exceptional act in an exceptional circumstance. The liberation and creativity this state allows would be a stark contrast with the state of living that most human beings accept as normal.

Yet this state can also arise in our everyday lives. If we could be in the state of *fana fi afal* life would reveal itself as miraculous.

The third stage is *fana fi dhat*. This may appear as the easiest of the three stages after we have passed through the first two. It is definitely a much more profound state. In this state, we see even ourselves as a gift. The Andalusian Sufi mystic, poet, and philosopher Ibn Arabi expressed this beautifully when he said,

> My spiritual journey was entirely within my own being. But when I came to the presence of my Lord and Sustainer, I saw that I was nothing but servanthood, without a trace of sovereignty.

The key to all three stages is servanthood. The *realization* of it is servanthood. The third stage is very close to the state known

---
55. *Surah al-Anfal* 8:17.

as *jam*. In some Eastern traditions it might be envisioned that this state, known in their path as *nirvana*, is the goal of everything. Nirvana is held out as the ultimate accomplishment. *Jam* is not the goal of the Sufi journey, however, but a station on the way. (In the Mevlevi *sema* the third *salaam* is *jam*. The fourth *salaam* in the *sema* is the stage beyond *jam*.) One can't live in the state of *fana fi dhat*. In fact, if we have a *murshid*, and we reach *fana fi dhat*, he may well pull us out of that stage and hang us out to dry.

Experiencing the bliss of oneness makes a person too intoxicated to be functional. This could be seen in Rama Krishna's behavior in certain moments. God bless him, this is not a criticism. He was great and enlightened, but he couldn't put his socks on at times. In our Tradition, we want to be able to put our socks on.

After this is the stage that is referred to as *Hazrati Jam*. It means "the presence of *jam*." *Hazrati Jam* is the period of getting over being enlightened. I use the term "enlightened" very loosely. I think what is meant by the name is, "You've been in *jam*, now we're going to drag you into presence. We're going to derive a presence from that *jam*, or unification, and you're just going to chill out for a while. You're going to get your self back and you're going to get used to having a self again." It's a very delicate stage and it could be one which lasts a long time. For some people, it could be a period of re-education. It is possible for somebody to go into the *jam* too soon and without proper preparation. This usually won't happen under the guidance of a *murshid*, but it can happen accidentally. Some people win the spiritual lottery and get drawn into that selflessness. It's typically terrifying when it happens in this way. It's not terrifying, or even dramatic if it's done in the typical stages of Sufi education. For some people it can be a rather natural process of maturing and may be almost unnoticeable in some respects. There is a gradual disengagement from the false self and engagement with something else. There are moments of bliss and union connected to an experience of the essential self. In this

How the False self Dissolves

experience, one pole of our being is a finite self and the other is infinite nonexistence.

On the Sufi path, your spirit would be ready for this state because you have been both educated and trained for it as well as having been in *zhikr* and *sema* enough. With such preparation, entry into the state happens gracefully.

The final stage is called *Jam ul Jam*. This is a state of deep maturity and ordinariness. It is characterized by fully embracing a self that lives like an ordinary human being. In some sense, this stage is never separate from the awareness of our reciprocal communion and intimacy with the Divine. It doesn't mean that one is free from suffering. It doesn't mean that one doesn't make mistakes. There is, however, an entirely different experience of individuality. Our individuality in *Jam ul Jam* never loses trust and gratitude or sight of the beauty of the Divine in everything.

Internal and External Waystations on the Path

The Seeker will Appear in the Sought

SOMETIMES WE HAVE TO DISCOVER our heart through something outside ourselves. Experiences of devotion come easily within certain external frameworks, like holy places in Turkey, the Mevlevi tradition's homeland. The challenge is to sustain some of that orientation every day.

In speaking about *Hajj*, the Muslim pilgrimage to Mecca, the Mevlevi tradition says the *Kaaba*, the shrine pilgrims circle in Mecca, is the heart of the perfected human being and that the *Kaaba* is actually in our hearts. Mecca, Medina, the Dome of the Rock, Sultanahmet Mosque, Mevlana's *turbe*, Shams's *masjid*—are all outer places, but they are also all realities within us. In this manner, we build the inner *masjid*, mosque, the inner *turbe*, tomb shrine, and the inner *tekke*, dervish lodge.

All of these places are waystations on the road to the Divine Presence. At the same time, that Divine Reality is not a far-off destination. It's available to us right here and now.

Mevlana beautifully advises us to start fresh and to open—or to open *more*—to Divine Reality:

> By the mercy of God, Paradise has eight doors. One of those is the door of repentance, child. All the others are sometimes open, sometimes shut. But the door of repentance is never closed. Come, seize the opportunity! The door's open. Carry your baggage there at once!
> Though your life has almost passed, this present moment is its root. If it lacks moisture, water it with repentance.

Water the root of this present moment with repentance. Give the living water to the root of your life, so that the tree of your life may flourish. By this water, past mistakes are redeemed. By this water last year's poison is made sweet.

Give the living water to the root of your life so that the tree of your life may flourish.

Repentance creates a framework for devotion. In our spiritual practices, we dip into the Higher Dimensional Reality of which we are a part. The perspective of that other Reality—*Haqq*, or the Creative Truth—remains with us. Everyday life is experienced within the context of devotion to the *Dost*—that Higher Dimensional Reality known as the Beloved or the Beloved Friend, which is loving, harmonizing, healing, and redeeming.

Shams tells us that "the sign of the Sought is already on the forehead of the seeker." A passage shows the *murid* being the seeker and also the one who is wishing, desiring, and longing for Unity and then becomes the *murad* (the one who is willed by God.)

Who is Seeking Who

In addition to these shaikhs of the outside who are famous among people and who are talked about from pulpits and gatherings, there are hidden servants more perfected than the famous ones. And there is One Who is Sought among them whom some do find. Mevlana thinks I am That but I don't think so. If I am not the Sought One, I am the seeker. In the end, the seeker raises his head also amid the Sought. God is seeking me now, but the story of that Sought One has not become famous in any book; nor is it spoken about among the orders. These words are all to tell you about the Path, and no one else speaks about it like this.

Shams tells us the one who is useful to others is doing what needs to be done.

True Assistance

Maybe a blasphemer is carrying water on the path, and there is someone who needs water. When the water comes to that person, he doesn't turn around to question where it came from, but right away his insides relax owing to that water. On the day of reckoning, that blasphemer will hold the hand of 100,000 Muslims. The work of God is beyond reason. One man may spend 200 silver coins for the dervishes and it has no effect, while five silver coins given by someone else prove more useful.

If it were possible to understand these meanings by study and discussions, then the best thing to do would be to put dust on one's head, and on Bayazid's and Junayd's and apprentice to Fakhr-i Razi for a hundred years. They say that in writing his commentaries on the Qur'an he used a thousand rolls of paper. Others say that he wrote 500 reams, but 100,000 Fakhr-i Razis can't approach even the dust of the path of Bayazid. Fakhr-i Razi is like the knocker on the door—and not on the inner door of the house, but rather the knocker on the outside door. The special part of the house where the sultan is secluded with his favorites is something else.

Mevlana's "It is Thou" from the *Masnavi* describes this process of spiritual wayfaring in more detail. In it we see how unity is possible but absence and separation may be needed first.

It is Thou

A certain man came and knocked at a friend's door.
His friend asked him, "Who is there?"
He answered, "It's me."
The friend said, "Go away, it's not the time.
There is no place for the raw at this table."
What will cook the raw one
except for the fire of absence and separation?
What will deliver him from hypocrisy?

The wretched man went away,
and for a year he traveled—in separation

from his friend he burned with sparks of fire.
That burned one was slowly cooked,
until he returned and again paced back and forth
before the house of his friend.

With mindful shyness he knocked at the door,
so no word of disrespect might escape from his lips.
"Who is at the door?" his friend called,
"It is Thou, O charmer of hearts," he answered.
"Now," said the friend, "since thou art I, come in, O myself:
there was never room in this house for two I's."

[*Masnavi* I: 3056–63]

Hope, Activity, and Awe

The interpretation of a sacred text is true
if it stirs you to hope, activity, and awe.

[*Masnavi* V, 3125–30]

RUMI'S *Masnavi* was written in the Persian language. The Persian word for "awe" means something like "bashfulness." "Modesty" is not an accurate meaning of the word for "awe." "Shame" is not either because the Persian word has no negative connotation. The meaning is also not the "awe" implied in a statement like, "O God! You're just so majestic!"

Rather, the word refers to a quality of being within ourselves that is without any presumption. It is being fully aware of our responsibility toward the Divine. Yet how presumptuous we often are and how infrequently might we feel our nothingness in relationship to the Divine instead. This theme is included in the following passages from Book Five of Rumi's *Masnavi*:

> The interpretation of a sacred text is true if it stirs you to
>   hope, activity, and awe.
> And if it makes you slacken your service, know the real truth
>   to be this:
> that it's a distortion of the sense of the saying, not a true
>   interpretation.
> This saying has come down to inspire you to serve,
> that God may take the hands of those who have lost hope,
>   and deliver them.
> Ask the meaning of the Qur'an from the Qur'an alone,
> and from that one who has set fire to his idle fancy and
>   extinguished it
> and has become a sacrifice to the Qur'an, bowing low in
>   humbleness,

so that the Qur'an has become the Essence of his Spirit, that essential oil that has wholly devoted itself to the rose. You can either smell that oil or the rose as you please.

[*Masnavi* V, 3125–30]

"Hope" is not what some have called "the disease of tomorrow." It's not a form of sleep implied by statements like "Tomorrow, I'll get around to it." "Tomorrow I will strengthen my spiritual practice." "Tomorrow I will find my discipline." "Tomorrow I will do what I don't feel like doing today, maybe." Although commonly experienced, that's not the kind of hope that is being talked about in the above passages from Rumi. The hope Mevlana is referring to is the hope that leads you to action, right now. It's conscious hope. It's what awakens us to act, to do.

Various Sufis and teachers of many faiths refer to hope at the level known as religion, or, in Islam, *shariah*. At this level, statements about hope typically include: "I'm going to pray and do all the proper practices with the hope that I won't be overly punished for my sins." "I'm going to do such and such and maybe God won't punish me. Perhaps I'll be rewarded with something beautiful in heaven, or maybe even in this life." That's hope at the level of *shariah* or religion.

Mevlana's guidance that we "ask the meaning of the Qur'an from the Qur'an alone" goes against what a lot of people are saying today. Many believe you don't have a right to interpret the Qur'an unless you have specific degrees from certain institutions, or know this *madhab*, this school of Islamic law, et cetera. I know I'm being controversial in making this point, but so is Mevlana. The guidance doesn't mean any ignorant person can start interpreting the Qur'an based on their own whims. The first two lines of the passage provide necessary considerations to guide our personal work with the Qur'an. "The interpretation of a sacred text is true, if it stirs you to hope, activity, and awe."

Hope at the level of *tariqah*, or the level of the esoteric path, is not dogma or doctrine. *Tariqah* is the level at which we in this

Tradition work. Hope at the level of *tariqah* underlies statements such as "I'm going to do my best to awaken as well as be conscious and aware, so that my *nafs*, the false self, will not get the better of me. I do this to avoid being so asleep that I stumble into foolish actions, negativity, and judgmental thoughts."

At the level of *tariqah*, the concept of "hope" is all about consciousness and awareness. That's the basis of what we're doing. It's not that we discard the first level that I mentioned. But there's something subtler going on because we understand that our hope is in awakening awareness. Without that, we're just following, almost automatically, outer morals and ethics. It's typical to begin a spiritual path with outer beliefs and little to no awareness or real consciousness. However, the spiritual path we are on is about awakening awareness. At the level of *tariqah*, it's doing all the practices and using the knowledge that leads the human being to self-awareness as well as to awareness in relationship. The latter is known as *adab*, spiritual courtesy.

"Hope" at the level of *haqiqah*, which is Divine Reality and Truth, is to be freed of the *nafs*. It is letting go of everything that impedes the manifestation of Divine Attributes, Divine Intelligence, and Divine Qualities. We never would say that you take the self completely away. There's always a self and an "I." This is true except in rare moments. In general, there's always a sense of "I" in our everyday life. At the level of *haqiqah*, hope is to live free of those aspects of the self that lead to negativity, including fear, blame, and judgment. These lead to the wrong kind of self-consciousness, doubt, and withholding, which in turn, obscure and get in the way of the Divine Intelligence's reflection. This reflection should be coming through every human being, breath by breath. "Hope," at the level of *haqiqah*, at the level of Reality, is to live so that *ar-Rahman*, the Infinite Compassion, is seated on the Throne of your Heart.

The orientation Mevlana provides is not to something external, a set of beliefs, or even less, a set of prescriptions and rules. Prescriptions and rules are not bad. But Mevlana is teaching us at the level of *haqiqah* and *tariqah*. A person who approaches the Qur'an in humility can potentially change their human spirit to send out into the world the essence of the Divine, just as essential oil takes on the fragrance of the rose. It's the same fragrance, whether you smell the oil or the rose. What an extraordinary thing to imagine a human being becoming the essence of the revelation.

We have encountered this transformation through our *murshids*, or teachers. We fell in love with them because of that love. We fell in love with the fragrance of the rose. We didn't fall in love with any beliefs, doctrine, dogma, or even religion. We felt the transmission of what comes to "one who has set fire to his idle fancy and extinguished it." The idle fancy of the *nafs* that says, "I'll get around to it tomorrow," "If only I didn't have to work so hard," "If only I didn't have a family," "If only it weren't the twenty-first century", or, "If only I lived in some traditional society, where I could be spiritual." These statements imply a perception that things were different and easier in the past.

The following quote about hope is from the Qur'an.

> *And offer them the parable of the life of this world. It's like the water which We send down from the skies and which is absorbed by the plants of the earth. But in time they turn into dry stubble, which the winds blow freely about. And it is God who determines all things. Wealth and children are an adornment in this world's life. But the acts of wholeness and reconciliation, the fruits of which abide forever, are of far greater merit in your Sustainer's sight and a far better source of hope.*

[*Surah al-Kahf*, 18:45–46]

As often happens, the Qur'an brings us down to essentials. On its face, the message of *Surah* 18 does not appear to be a mystical assertion. But, upon reflection, we see that it is.

This *surah* from the Qur'an is telling us to undertake acts of wholeness and reconciliation because the resulting fruits abide forever. As precious as our children are, the acts we are encouraged to undertake create something that our wealth and even our children do not. Acts of wholeness and reconciliation are eternal because they are of a spiritual substance. They're an outer action, but their reality is on a spiritual level.

I suggest a practical activity that is in alignment with this idea of hope involving action. I suggest you take up a notch whatever your spiritual practice is and enjoy it more. Strengthen your practice, appreciate it, be thankful for it, and take pleasure in it.

Developing Will and the Nature of Attainments

ONE OF THE IMPORTANT ELEMENTS in this Universe is the element of choice. Having the ability to choose, especially between right and wrong, as well as good and evil, is considered a great Divine gift. The Divine Revelations speaking to human beings on our level, and especially the Qur'an, emphasize the matter of choice. We can follow the implications of having that choice into very deep and profound reflections. Thomas Merton, for example, said, "Your greatest possibility is to be what God created you to be."

Some people will play around with the idea that there really is no choice. If you get too mystical you can get yourself into a universe where there seems to be no choice. But another way to get to a place where there is no choice is when you just utterly surrender to Divine Will. You can live in a permanent state of flow and a pure "yes" where there is no choice.

This is an incredible possibility and a contrast to choosing something quite banal. The characteristic of an awakened human being is one who has will. The Tradition defines will as "having the power of conscious choice." To be able to exercise your will is to be able to make a choice in any moment. Giving up your self, or what the self wants, is a very high choice.

The awakening of will on the spiritual path is always emphasized as one of the lines of development for us. In Sufism, something is called an "attainment" if we can do it at will. In the beginning of just opening up to the spiritual path everyone experiences having no control over being present. Little by little, we come to value being present and choose the things that develop presence. In time, presence becomes more of a choice and an attainment. Choosing things that develop presence is almost like exercising.

Spiritual development happens when we learn to do certain things at will. Jesus said, "Love." Can we choose to love at will? What might seem impossible at first can be attained in small steps. Can you practice loving a house plant, for instance? And then you might graduate to loving a pet. Eventually, you might find it possible to love even some "unloveable" human beings.

Another important attainment is forgiveness. In this moment, forgiveness at will may not be possible for many of us. Maybe we would like to forgive, but we can't. Perhaps suddenly one day forgiveness may come without our will. It may then be possible to develop that capacity for forgiveness, or love, or the capacity to be present.

As an exercise in presence, it is a very good practice to reverse our vision and allow ourselves to be seen. The Prophet gave a beautiful example of this when he defined *ihsan*, which means "beautiful righteousness." The Prophet said, "*Ihsan* is to live as if you saw the Divine right in front of you, and if you don't, to know that you are seen." This creates a different state in us. If we cannot see the Divine in front of us, we can at least experience being seen. We can choose a moment, maybe an hour in the week, for the practice of being seen by the Divine. If we experience a little forgetfulness in that moment of being seen then we can return to being seen as we remember our intention and choice. In that moment of presence we may also reflect on what we are holding in our hearts at that point in time. What are we using this precious substance of life for? What are our thoughts, our desires, or our actions in that moment of being seen? What are we doing with our lives in that moment of being seen? We can have enough positive self-esteem to look at ourselves critically and maybe see something new. Maybe we will see our greed, laziness, anger, fear, or pride.

There is another understanding to witnessing that Mevlana shares with us: "On the Day of Resurrection your hands will be witnesses against you." Whatever we did with our hands during our lives will testify either against us or for us. The function of a witness is not just to see but also to reveal the truth. What if we could be that kind of witness? We could be witnesses for the Highest Truth we know. This is big. Are we willing to be witnesses for that Highest Truth? Are we ready to be the kind of person for whom, when we are present, more Truth is present? In such a case, there is less ego and less of "my" likes, "my" wants and "my" preferences. We could then somehow bring into every situation that which helps others to get free of themselves.

A real dervish is one who glorifies God deeply and lives in that state of glorification. How do we glorify God? We can inwardly remember the Divine through the Names of God. We can maybe call *"Ya Wadud! Ya Wadud! Ya Wadud!"* ("O Loving One! O Loving One! O Loving One!") or *"Ya Hayy! Ya Hayy! Ya Hayy!"* ("O Ever Living One! O Ever Living One! O Ever Living One!") or *"Ya Latif!"* ("O You who are so subtle in all the ways You give to us!") or *"Ya Ghafur!"* ("O You who love to forgive more than anybody in the Universe can forgive!"). We need to know this forgiveness for our forgetfulness. The dervish who glorifies God becomes a witness. Where is the evidence of that glorification? Does it show if you claim to glorify God? Does it transmit?

We see it in the face. We feel it as a light coming out of the dervish's eyes. We see radiance surround the dervish and we feel it. Mevlana tells us:

> The gnostic's glorification of God is perfect, for her feet and hands have borne witness to her glorification. It has lifted her up from the dark pit of the body and redeemed her from the bottom of the dungeon of this world. On her shoulder is the sign of glorification, the silken robe of piety, and a light which surrounds her. She is delivered from the transitory world and she is dwelling in the Rose Garden and therein is a running Fountain. Her sitting place and home and abode is on the Throne of the highest aspiring inmost consciousness and her station is the seat of sincerity. All of the *Siddiq*, the truly sincere ones, are flourishing and joyous. Their faces are fresh. Their praise, like the garden's praise on

account of Spring, has a hundred signs and a hundred glories. Fountains and palms and herbs and rosebeds and plots of bright-colored flowers bear witness to this Springtime. Everywhere thousands of witnesses to the Beloved are bearing testimony as the pearl bears witness to the oyster's shell.

[*Masnavi* IV 1763–74]

Have we ever had a glimpse of that Reality or a taste of that Gratitude or felt blessed by that Beloved? What would we do with it?

The work of choice involves taking from that world of transcendent beauty and funneling it into this world through beautiful character, justice, and peace.

Mevlana says, "A single prostration is worth more than the Universe and all it contains." We should touch the Reality of that statement. A true prostration is worth more than the Universe and all it contains.

The way to that moment is through the diligent and sometimes boring work of patiently dealing with our *nafs* as it arises. This is where we are a lot of the time. So we are probably familiar with the work of self-observation. But there is also this other work of glorification and being in love with the Beloved. This is the work of gratitude.

Mevlana was drunk with it. A dervish should breathe it and live for it. A dervish can know that joy. When the dervish is sorrowful and in contraction she accepts the knowing that sooner or later the contraction will become expansion.

Sometimes we will be given that gift of a transcendent experience if we practice and give enough time to it. It is not so far away. It is not so veiled. That Beauty does not wish to be so concealed. That Beauty is not distancing Itself from us.

The Inner Life: Aspects of the Heart

ON THE PATH OF SUFISM, the work is about a balance between the outer and the inner. This means an inner that is not just thoughts and emotions that are a reaction to what is outer, but an inner that is relatively free, empty, and spacious. It is just the beginning of a lifelong experience, a journey of coming to know what is of real value. A journey to Truth that is beyond theologies and human concepts. A Truth that is known and verified through our own experience of finding the relationship with the inner life and the outer life. We experience how the inner life can complement, enhance, and give meaning to our outer life.

There are quite precise, clearly differentiated levels of experience of this inner world, terms that are described in the Qur'an and are known to the Sufis.

The first term would be translated as the breast or chest. The word in Arabic is *sadr*. Often, it's translated just as "heart." All the words referred to can be translated as heart, in the sense that the heart represents the Whole. But this first word *sadr*, refers to a level of experience that is close to our emotional life, our inner whisperings, our contractions and expansions, emotionally. Let us call it the chest.

Awareness can enter the breast and experience what is going on there. This experience has great dimensions of joy, sorrow, happiness, disturbance, and a whole realm of ourselves. Yet it is still one of the superficial levels of our inner life.

God says in the Qur'an's *Surah ash-Sharh, Have we not expanded your chest? And removed from you the burdens which had weighed down your back?*[56] The Divine can come into the human inner realm, and expand it, purifying it.

---

56. *Surah ash-Sharh* 94:1–3.

One level deeper than *sadr* is called *qalb*, which is the heart, properly speaking. The extraordinary thing about the heart is that it is not under the command of the self. Although we can do things that affect the heart's health, vibrancy, and awakeness, the heart is still under the command of the Divine. You can ignore it, cover it over, or obscure it, but it is essentially, as one colleague said, the "Embassy of God" within your being. How beautiful the heart is, if we were truly to understand it. How beautiful that it's within all of us.

If our lives are externalized, and preponderantly about material desires, ambitions, ego-satisfactions, and pursuit of immediate gratifications, there are all kinds of dangers. If our main concerns are getting by in this world, dealing with our responsibilities, holding a job, showing up for the job, finishing the job, and things we have to do, it is a pity. The least danger of such a life is that it will result in superficiality and triviality.

To know the heart, to sense the state and guidance of the heart, requires an ability to clear some space within ourselves. It requires an ability to focus our attention, within our own being. It would be good to have some time each day where we're totally turned within. Doing so, however, is not at the exclusion of the outer life.

The practice is to have a simultaneous awareness of outer and inner. It is to be in relationship with the outer, but to have an empty space within ourselves, and to be awake, in presence and openness. An inner openness that allows us to live our lives while really paying attention, and at the same time, having an openness in that inner direction. This allows us to catch those subtle impulses that come to us. We receive the subtle Intelligence that operates within us, the Divine Guidance and promptings of our Divine Friend. This is *qalb*, the heart.

The next deeper level is the within-ness of the heart. It could be called the inner heart. In Arabic and in the Qur'an it's referred to as *fu'ad*. If the heart itself is knowing, *fu'ad* itself is seeing. *Fu'ad* is a deeper knowing, an inner heart. Another important word related to *fu'ad* is *ihsan*, and it can be translated as perfect benevolence or perfect goodness. It's defined by Prophet Muhammad as worshipping God as if we saw Him. Worship is not limited to the ritual prayers in the mosque; it extends to reverencing and serving God in every moment of our lives, as if we see the Divine right in front of us.

To be realistic, very few people are like that, so the next best thing is to know that *we are seen*. It's not a creepy feeling that God is watching us with the intention of finding some mistake for which we should be punished. That is what a religion of fear might teach. For Sufis, knowing that we are seen has a beautiful meaning.

It is a reversal of space, a subtle shift of perception. Normally we are locked into our own viewpoint, always looking at the world through "my" vision and "my" perspective. Imagine that we could just let go of that and allow ourselves to be seen, as if space is looking at us. This is a shift of being. It's not a self-consciousness that we're talking about. It's just allowing ourselves to be seen, because we realize we are within the presence of an Infinite Intelligence that is nurturing, full of blessing, generosity, and guidance. We're cared for.

The best stage is to live, worship, and serve as if we see God in front of us all the time. But the second-best stage is living in the knowledge we are held in a vision of the Divine.

The beautiful state of *ihsan* is what the Prophet Muhammad passed on to us. The most beautiful state for a human being is to live every breath as if we see the Divine, the Face of God, everywhere. If we can't do that, at least be in that state where we feel that sort of fastidiousness that comes when we intend to live beautifully. We intend not to wound others' hearts. We intend to do things in the most beautiful way. For this deeper state of the inner heart, *fu'ad*, a different way of seeing is necessary.

The fourth level, in Arabic, is *lubb*. *Lubb* means the kernel of something, like the nutritious essence of a nut. The *lubb* of the soul, of the human being, is a very, very deep and essential knowing. It is even deeper than *fu'ad*, the inner heart. If *fu'ad* is the pupil of the eye, *lubb* is the light that allows the eye to see. There is something that is flowing into our inner life from Spirit, from the Divine. It brings with it an insightful knowingness that is like reason on such a sublime level that we know what action is most appropriate. We receive a kind of guidance, in each moment, as when we sometimes know, see, and act with a high level of reason. It is not a mental, analytical reason. It is a knowingness that supports our action, and even our thoughts. It is a deep, insightful knowingness from something even deeper than the inner heart.

Going back to *sadr*, the chest, the beautiful *surah* in the Qur'an that starts by asking, *Have we not expanded your chest?* The Divine comes in and opens us up as it enters through the heart and into the chest. In the Qur'an it says the beautiful quality of faith can be inscribed on our *sadr*, on our whole being, making our whole emotional lives different. Instead of being governed by resentment, pride, and fear, there's an opening. *Sadr* is the most superficial level.

The next level, *qalb*, the heart, the Embassy of the Divine within our being, belongs to the Divine Source. The Prophet Muhammad said, "There is something within the body, and when it is healthy and whole, then the whole body is healthy and whole." When the heart is sound, all of our other functions—our intelligence, emotions, and even our physical body—are sound. So much depends on the quality of our hearts. That is why Sufism is above all the science of the purification of the heart. This purification aims to free the heart of all envy, resentment, and false pride.

Being proud in a holy way is possible, but what we mean by pride is thinking we're superior to others or looking down on others. Envy is not envying someone who has something beautiful and good, but to wish they didn't have it and that we had it instead. It's a negative state to envy the holy. An example is seeing someone who is truly kind, good, and generous, truly with God and finding that annoying. That's envy.

Resentment is that low, simmering dissatisfaction that we hardly recognize, about the circumstances of our lives, and the people we share our life with, and the world we're in. It's a very unhealthy state.

All of these things can be blown away with the breast purified by the Divine through the heart which is with God, the inner heart. The inner heart not only knows, it also sees deeply.

Every person on a spiritual journey will go through certain levels. These are levels through which we see. We don't all look from the same level. We move through different levels with our vision—sometimes fairly high, sometimes fairly low—and we need to know this as part of our inner life.

We can see how much depends on the inner life when our hearts become purified, and our vibration and levels of perception change. If we're looking at the world and everything looks mean and ugly on certain days, that's us, not the world. On other days we walk outside and fall in love with everything we see, praise be to God. That's another level. It occurs when we are seeing through the Divine's eyes.

The inner vision, the *fu'ad*, encompasses the levels of seeing that we're capable of and that can be deeper, higher, and at the same time more inward.

And finally, there is *lubb*. *Lubb* comes as a beautiful gift, the kernel of insight that can be so profound, perfect, and beautiful that it informs every action, thought, movement, and word.

This is why we need an inner life. If we only have an outer life, we will never be satisfied or happy. To be totally preoccupied with the outer life can never satisfy, bring peace to the heart, or bring us to the true happiness that we as human beings are meant to experience. Spirituality is the most important part of life because our true happiness and state of wellbeing comes from our ability to be in contact with a state of timelessness and perfection that is beyond all circumstance and conditions. This is what we're meant to and can know, through opening up the inner life and allowing it to meet the outer life, as well as by deepening through all these levels. The inner life—the journey within—is really a journey back to our Source and what we essentially are. It is calling us because It wants us to know Its love, generosity, and beauty.

Mevlana Rumi often talks about the development of this kind of spiritual perception.

> Since our vision is so limited,
> let our sight be dissolved in the seeing of the Friend.
> Our sight for His, what an exchange!
>
> [*Masnavi* I, 921-22]

> Though the Universes are 18,000 and more,
> not every eye can see them.
> Every atom is indeed the place of the vision of God,
> but as long as it is unopened,
> who says there is a door?
>
> [*Masnavi* I, 3756, 3766]

In the Qur'an there's a chapter called the "The Bee." A part of the message of that chapter is that the work of making honey for the bees in their hives results from Divine inspiration: *And God revealed to the bees.* Revelation for the bees was how to make honey. What, then, is the revelation for the human being? Here is what Rumi has to say:

> What God taught to the bees
> doesn't belong to the lion or wild ass.
> The bees make a home of juicy sweetness—
> God opened the door of that knowing.
>
> What God taught the silkworm—
> does any elephant have such expertise?
> Adam, though made of earth,
> was given knowledge by God,

a knowledge like light
that pierced the Seven Heavens.

[*Masnavi* I, 1009–12]

It's this knowledge and inner knowing that characterizes human beings, a knowledge like Light.

Be An Impartial Witness

TO SAY, "Be an objective witness, see *Hu* everywhere," does not mean it is possible to do that all the time, every minute of the day. There may be times when we dive into creativity or are living directly in a state of freedom. When we get involved with political, economic, and even romantic situations which are of personal concern to us, it might be hard to be totally impartial witnesses. However, there are times, too, where it may be appropriate to try to be an objective witness. "Impartial" would be a better word.

How do we contextualize "to see *Hu* everywhere" in our own way or choose to understand these words?

There is a spiritual model, a cosmology of the self, from a Sufi perspective that can help guide us.

This thing that we call "self" or "I" is made up of cultural or familial conditioning. Our experience of "I" can be understood as running along a continuum. At lower levels on this spectrum some of us may know addictive behaviors and be enslaved by desires, feelings, and any number of things in this world. At a level slightly above these lower levels, we have action based on selfish desire. At a level a little bit higher, we have action based on the healthy, balanced desire of an integrated, mature human being. At one end of this spectrum, then, is the conditioned self and at the other end is Spirit. At the Spirit end is an experience of timelessness, eternal presence, equanimity, impartiality, unconditional love, and pure witnessing. This whole spectrum is the "self." It is an experience of I-ness at all the different levels possible for a human being to know. We may not be at the Spirit end of the spectrum very often. Sometimes we are lucky just to be at the level of a healthy, sane, and functional human being. That in itself would be quite an achievement for most people in this crazy world.

Be an Impartial Witness

In our spiritual work we practice meditation and remembrance. Remembrance is done by reciting the Names of God aloud or silently. We also worship. Worship involves presence in our movement and a reverential communion with the Divine. We work and are of service in the world. We have community and relationships. All of these spiritual activities and the knowledge that goes along with these things are aimed at helping us be conscious along the spectrum of the self. To be an impartial witness is a pretty high point on this continuum.

The human being is a paradox because we are both earthly and heavenly. In Sufism we accept that a certain amount of human desire is good. We learn from the constant efforts we exert as we try to achieve our desires, whether we actually achieve them or not. Sometimes, we may succeed in achieving what we desire and quickly find out that true happiness is not in attaining every desire that arises in us. When we attain what we had hoped to with our lives, we begin to get the idea that wellbeing and contentment are not totally dependent on circumstances. It is separate from what we manage to attain, have, or own.

The practice of referencing regularly the higher levels of the human spectrum that are possible can help us see more of the Divine everywhere. From the vantage point of the higher self and Spirit, we see more plainly the qualities of the Divine manifesting in the ordinary. We see the interplay of life and relationships. We see the Divine teaching us.

Most of us are trying to take care of ourselves and possibly others. We have relationships in which we want to be responsible and engaged. We want to be good in the roles that make up our life. These may include being a good citizen, husband, son, or father. All these things are potentially good.

As we mature and live a spiritual life, we begin to experience and see, whether implicitly or explicitly, that something is possible for us that is not dependent on circumstance, possessions, praise, blame, or what the world thinks of us. This possibility is our connection with a state of unconditional wellbeing and happiness.

In Sufism, the point is not to give up the self. It certainly is not to kill the self. Instead, we are to transform the self through the levels of the spectrum I've described. By doing so, we begin to live at a level where we can let go in life. We trust life and act from the heart. This is an art.

At the lower level of the human experience we are conditioned creatures who may also have inner contradictions. These could include repressed anger, selfishness, defensiveness, prejudice, and arrogance, to name a few psychological obstacles. Psychotherapy can help to recondition the conditioned self with emotional healing. When there are moral and religious teachings, along with the work of ethics, these can also help us to purify the conditioned self and the conditioned heart.

The work of mysticism is somewhere else along that spectrum. We understand that the mystical states are dependent on a good ethical foundation and built upon being a healthy, balanced human being. There are so many things the great mystics have taught about overcoming obstacles to listening to and acting from the heart.

Mevlana says, "With one answer God answers a hundred questions." When Spirit comes into the human "self" it has a way of transforming that "self" to make people spontaneously good and spontaneously generous, rather than super-ego "good." This is a model that we keep coming back to and repeating in different ways all the time. Gradually we begin to experience ourselves as rising to a level where we are resonating with the Merciful, Impartial Awareness. The more we move up to that level, the more we arrive in that Divine Reality whose nature is fundamentally Compassionate, Merciful, Loving, Generous, and Beautiful. Since like attracts like, the human being who is resonating and conscious at that level sees deeply into this existence and perceives that which corresponds to this Inner Beauty. Similarly, if we slip down the scale into a state of fear, defensiveness, anxiety, suspicion, confusion, and doubt, what we perceive in the world is very likely going to correspond to that perception. Like attracts like. Since the states at the conditioned end of the spectrum are fundamentally distorted by the partiality and the prejudice of the ego, the perception of Reality is distorted. At the lowest level it is pure delusion and insanity.

There was a great Sufi named Abdul-Qadir al-Jazairi who lived in nineteenth century Algeria. He was an incredible man of action. He worked for social justice for the minorities in that country in that time. He led a rebellion against French colonialism. He is a great hero of North Africa. He was also a great mystic in the tradition of Ibn Arabi. He deserves to be respected as one of the great Sufi mystics and military leaders in history. As an Algerian military leader, he was a signatory to a treaty between the French and the Algerians. The French commander who received Abdul-Qadir wrote, "He reminds us of Jesus. He is thin and pale but luminous and he conducts himself like Jesus."

The reflections of Abdul-Qadir al-Jazairi are quite profound. They are based on and grow out of his knowledge of the Akbarian tradition of Sufism and Ibn Arabi.

In the last chapter of his book, *The Spiritual Writings of Emir Abdul-Qadir*, there is something that can deepen our conversation. The chapter is called "Unitive and Separative Vision." It is about vision within multiplicity. There is the vision of Unity, Oneness, and *Hu*. In contrast, there is the vision of multiplicity. This vision of the existence in which we live includes all the interplay of good and bad, right and wrong, pleasure and pain, inner and outer, as well as meaning and form.

Abdul-Qadir al-Jazairi begins by referring to the following statement made by the Prophet Muhammad, upon whom be peace and blessings: "Moments of oppression overcome my heart, then I ask forgiveness of God, and return towards Him repenting more than one hundred times a day."

Abdul-Qadir al-Jazairi comments on this statement:

… this saying designates a covering of clothing and whether this covering be of the order of sensible things or spiritual realities as is the case here, it happens in fact that there are certain moments the Prophet is crushed by the vision of the immensity of Divine Sovereignty and by what is implied by absolute servanthood.

The Prophet is crushed by his vision of God's Sovereignty and his own role as absolute servant of God. That is the servanthood which the Divinity of God requires.

For over fourteen centuries, Sufism has been an applied spirituality practiced in everyday life. It is a spirituality for people who assume responsibilities in the world and who do not withdraw from life. Sufism has always been a path in the midst of life. People who practice Sufism have a productive livelihood, family, and relationships, if these are in their destiny. Mysticism is learning to connect to the states of being which, at their highest level, are timeless and spaceless. Mysticism is an experience of transcendent purity that brings inspiration. That experience happens with a stillness that is energized. It creates within us an emptiness that is light and a quietness that is pregnant. This is the beautiful work of the mystic. This mysticism can advance the transformation of the conditioned self more quickly and more thoroughly than moral and religious teachings alone. Psychotherapy is one level of sorting out human problems that can be vital. But its outcome can be limited. At a certain level, spirituality comes in as the healer and transforms the soul from the inside out. It has this incredible power no matter what anybody's personal story may be.

The Word and the Name

WHAT WOULD HAPPEN to a human being who grew up in the wild, without any instruction in language? What would that person's inner life be like? There are such cases studied in linguistics classes. The stories are from the eighteenth or nineteenth century. They are about feral people who emerged from the forest, having lived their entire life among wild animals.

Of course, being a mammal brings with it certain positive qualities. Mammals have warmth and affection and they establish relationship without language. You do not need language for some of these things.

But there are certain things that you do need language for, such as intentionality and principles. Living by principles is what makes us human. We are not yet talking about the refinements of spiritual perception that Sufism works with. Just at the level of moral principles, there are things that cannot be a principle for a human being until they are conceived as a principle through language. Otherwise, if you don't have that, you are at the mercy of whichever way the winds blow.

It is important to use language consciously. In Western culture, we often use too many words. We speak them unconsciously. It's worse when we use them negatively or in an ugly way. The Mevlevi tradition is very careful about how to express things. It seems that somebody in the history of this lineage had a profound realization about the nature of language and its relationship to the sacred. As a result, Mevlevis really strive to embody this.

Mevlana says: "O tongue, you are an endless blessing! O tongue, you are an endless curse!"

Respecting the word inwardly and outwardly encourages us to develop this type of awareness. It means taking responsibility for your words, inwardly and outwardly. Every word that you put out in the Universe cannot be called back.

When first encountering a community like the Mevlevi, some of the language may sound unfamiliar. Over time, a number of the words and phrases become very meaningful and even vehicles for spirit. *Subhanallah, Alhamdulillah, Allahu Akbar*... This is the language of heaven, reminding us that the Divine is subtle beyond all-knowing (*Subhanallah*), ultimately beautiful and worthy of praise (*Alhamdulillah*), and greater than anything we can conceive (*Allahu Akbar*). It's mysterious. There is a blessing in words of a certain quality. They carry energy. They carry a state.

Many of the greatest saints of the great traditions have said it all comes down to the Word, the Divine Name. It's amazing how many of the mystics have reached that conclusion. They tell how there is nothing more than the Word. It is all there if we sincerely and consciously sustain remembrance through the Divine Name. When we achieve that, we are living within the level of the Divine Creative Power. It says in the Qur'an, Allah said *"Kun" ["Be"], and it is.*[57] Similarly, the Vedas say the Divine created by saying, *"Bhu!"* The Hindu shastras say: "From the sound of the Vedas the Supreme Divinity made all things."

Everything is made manifest through sound. In some sense, everything is sound. At a certain level, we can appreciate the sound and nature of everything. We can call this "worship," *zhikr*, "remembrance," or "prayer." All are intimately involved with sound and the power of the word.

A human being can develop sensitivities by listening to sound at the audible level as well as beyond that, on even more subtle levels. This deep listening helps us know that we inhabit the creative level of existence, whether we are conscious of it or not. Reality contains many levels and the human being encompasses them all. The beauty of sounds and the Divine Names is that we are in a holy universe of sound. The Divine

---

57. Variants of this phrase occur a number of times in the Qur'an, for example *Surah Ghafir* 40:68.

Word becomes our contact with Reality on all levels of this reality.

The Name or Word helps us to fix our consciousness on Reality. We can thereby renew our contact with the Inward Center and stabilize our communion with Spirit. As simple as that is, to have a tool that fixes our consciousness on Reality is no small thing. In *zhikr*, the remembrance of God through Divine Names, every word is a fresh impulse of Divine Reality as it keeps rhythmically repeating. Every pulse is a reconnection. It is something extraordinary.

As an exercise, you can choose a Divine Name to repeat in silence and stay with that Name long enough to experience it. Even though you may be with that Name in silence, there is still a sound that we can hear inwardly. The next part of this exercise is to unite the sound with Meaning. Realize they are not two things. They are one. If we could experience, understand, and practice this, the whole nature of our practice would deepen. When we do *salaat*, the ritual prayer, or *zhikr*, either aloud or silently, there is still Sound.

The words we hear and recite during prayer sometimes may open a space within us. At other times the recitation and sounds may be merely mental. This raises the question of why the ritual prayer has words. One of the reasons words are part of it is that if there were no words it would be harder to focus and we might be distracted by our own inner talking. The words and language are in a way preemptive. The language of worship stills the mind because it gives the mind something to focus on. Ideally, *salaat* gives the body, mind, and heart something to do so that a comprehensive state of presence might be experienced. There may come a time when one can pray in complete silence and simply stand behind the imam. This is allowed. It is beautiful to have an imam to stand behind. He or she says the words, and you are just there as an open-hearted presence.

Our experience of the Word depends on our receptivity. The United Church of Christ has a slogan, "God is still speaking." We may quickly acknowledge that yes, of course, God is still speaking. But the real question is, "Are we still listening?" Sometimes words seem mechanical and rote. They don't convey much at all when this is our perception of them. At other times, the exact words are richly meaningful. This has less to do with the words themselves than the state in which we are hearing the words.

Can you say "*Allah*," listen to the sound, and unite the sound with meaning? In the New Testament, we read: "Man does not live by bread alone, but by every Word that proceeds from the mouth of the Lord." This a perfect example and reminds us of the Qur'an. It is the Divine Word that nourishes us. Mevlana says this to us in many ways as well. The Word is nutriment and the food of our souls. Even the ancient Greeks knew this. Their metaphysics was not different from ours. The words for initiation into the Eleusinian Mysteries go back perhaps to 1,000 B.C. and tell us,

> So help me Heaven, with the work of God,
> who is great and wise.
> So help me, the Word of the Father, which he spoke when he established the whole universe in His wisdom.

In the Gospels, "Holy Breath" is the same as the "Holy Spirit," or *pneuma*. Master Eckhart, probably the greatest mystic of the West, tells us: "Father and Son expire Holy Breath. Once the Holy Breath inspires a man, It remains in him or her for he is essential and pneumatic."

Something that is very important here is that once the Holy Breath reaches a human, it stays there. With that embodied Breath, we become the Holy Spirit. They say in Sufism: "The *murid* is fed by the words of the *murshid* the words of *sohbet*."[58]

This refers to that same process of Spirit entering the soul. The food comes from the Divine when the Words have some connection with the Divine. It's another case of something

---

58. *Murid*: student. *Murshid*: master or teacher. *Sohbet*: spiritual conversation with the teacher.

entering the soul, transforming it, and remaining because the self has become spiritualized. There are intimate relationships between words, sound, meaning, and breath. The Qur'an says:

> *Are you not aware how God sets forth the parable of a Good Word? Like a good tree, firmly rooted with its branches towards the sky, yielding its fruit at all times, by its Sustainer's leave. And God propounds parables to men so that they might reflect.*
>
> [*Surah Ibrahim*, 14:24–25]

This tells us a good word is like a good tree. Its roots are firmly anchored, its branches reach to heaven, and it yields fruit.

> *And a corrupt word is like a corrupt tree, torn up from its roots, onto the face of the earth, wholly unable to endure. Thus God grants firmness unto those who have attained to faith through the Word that is unshakably true in the life of this world as well as in the life to come.*
>
> [*Surah Ibrahim*, 14:26–27]

This Parable of the Good Word also tells us that true words have an enduring power, but false words have no power in the long run. This is the way the Divine communicates to humanity. "Word" in this sense is something very creative, energetic, and powerful. It is not merely a conceptual formulation and opinion, but rather something from the Creative Source of existence itself.

The religion most people live is the fruit of a long tradition of logic, grammar, and rhetoric that is quite attenuated from what is real. They are branches of a tree with little reference to the source, the relationship, the devotion, and the love that inspired them. This is the corrupt tree that is torn up from its roots. God grants firmness to those who have attained faith through the Word, *Kalimah*. The "Word" refers to the Name that is unshakably true in the life of this world as well as in the life to come.

> *But the wrongdoers He lets go astray, for God does whatsoever He wills. Are thou not aware of those who have preferred a denial of the truth*

> *to God's blessings and invited their people to a like abode of utter desolation?*
>
> [*Surah Ibrahim*, 14:27–28]

We are getting a warning in this quote. There is always an option to choose to be focused on the blessings of Truth. This requires intention, effort, and faithfulness. Anything less than that has all kinds of hazards and potential for going astray or getting lost. It may also result in a darkening, misunderstanding, or wandering toward all the byways on which it is possible for a human being to wander on his or her ultimate way to the Truth.

When the Prophet Muhammad wanted to establish his rightful relationship to other religions, he said, "Let me call you to the *Kalimah as-Sawa*" or "the Reconciling Principle." *Kalimah*, is an Arabic word that means "word" as well as "principle." *Sawa* means "that which is equitable" or "that which is balanced." He said that principle, the *Kalimah as-Sawa*, would be, "Let us not have any lords other than God." Among the implications of this is that we not take other human beings as our masters, in preference to God. Let us unite on the very simple basis of recognizing this very basic Divine Reality. On that basis, we can respect each other.

These passages offer us possibilities for a practice that begins with an appreciation of the nature of sound, sound's relationship to meaning, and to the fact that we have been given Divine Names and Divine Words. The message allows us the possibility of spending time and living in that universe of holy sound.

We also have this possibility in music, singing *ilahis*, chanting, and recitation. We have the possibility in the *Masnavi*, Rumi's gift to us of his wisdom and teachings. That text is not, strictly speaking, a Divine Revelation. Nevertheless, it is an extraordinary holy text. All the more so if we can know some of it in Persian. Reading the *Masnavi* in Persian allows us to see the meanings that are there, for Persian, which is rich with Arabic vocabulary, is well suited for communicating spiritual truths.

The Word and the Name

All languages are holy. They are all from the Mother of Language. No language is profane unless it is used profanely. Every language is a gift from Allah. However, some languages are better suited for certain purposes than others. These purposes include the possibility of experiencing sacredness fully.

In the Qur'an, the word for the Divine Names is *Asma'*. The *Asma'* are also referred to as *Sifat*, "Qualities." *Asma'* can be the name of anything. *Lahul Asma' al-Husna*, from the Qur'anic *surah* "The Gathering," is one way the Divine Names are referred to. It translates as *to Him (Hu) belong the Most Beautiful Names*.[59] When God taught Adam, we read in the original language, He taught him *kalimah*. That is, the Divine sends words to us.

It's interesting to see how words are used in various contexts throughout the Qur'an. *Kalimah* occurs in the Qur'an in ways that are similar to its use in other parts of the Abrahamic tradition. For example, the most consistent use of the word *kalimah* in the Qur'an is when the word of God has brought about a transformation or judgment. It's always a kind of relationship, it's never just a label.

How can we gain a genuine relationship with the Divine Names? We can read about the Divine Names, but it seems that there will always be some mystery about them. The Names have a literal meaning as well as a sound signature that they carry. We can proceed in working with the Names having faith that each Name is imbued with a force and that this will unfold in the course of our practice.

Let's take one of the names like *al-Ba'ith*, the Resurrector, the One who Brings Back to Life, and the One who Puts Forth. When Jonah was *thrown forth from the whale* the word used in Arabic was *baitha*. We can learn about a Name like this intellectually, but it may be a while before we experience the reality of a Name as part of *zhikr*. It may take time for your conscious mind to understand or perceive the effects of that Name. Eventually, you may actually get to the point where

---

59. Surah al-Hashr 59:24.

something has been born from you, and you didn't know it. That is the action of *al-Ba'ith*.

For these Names to manifest requires what we call "your master desire." There must be devotion to the Name. It has to be invested with something. Then the results can be extraordinarily powerful. Your conscious mind may not even perceive those results immediately. Or there may not be an immediate cognitive sense of what a Name means until the effects have appeared in your life. Then, perhaps ten years later, you will look back on your life and exclaim, "How did I miss that? Why did I not see what, for example, *al-Baith* was bringing forth in my life? I was so in it, that I could not see it!"

Let's simplify even further and think of the name *Allah* or *Nur*. The human being who takes either of those Names and faithfully remembers God with them will, if there is some sincerity in the practice, be illuminated by those Names. The heart and self will be illuminated. The Name or Word helps us fix our consciousness on Reality, renewing our contact with the inward center, stabilizing our communion with Spirit.

This power to fix our consciousness on Reality is true of any of the Divine Names. The most comprehensive Divine Name, *Allah*, is sort of the multivitamin of the Divine Names. Remembrance with this Name will illuminate the heart and the entire being.

The human being who remembers God through the Divine Names will be a being who is in direct contact with God by opening that channel. There are glimmerings of meanings and feelings in what Divine Words and Divine Names inspire in us. It's not just something in the head, it's Life, it's a lived experience. Muhammad said, "The difference between one who does *zhikr* and one who doesn't is the difference between the living and the dead." The Name and the Named are one. It is not two. When you say the Name *you* are the Name.

Since returning from a trip to Turkey, a person shared that they had been working with the Divine Name of *al-Latif*. This person related how much more compelling, powerful, and mysterious the understanding of *Latif* is now compared to what they thought they understood about the name *Latif* before. One description of *Latif* refers to a subtlety that polishes and beautifies everything, including our heart and our *nafs* (self). Another person has shared what a powerful effect working with *ar-Razzaq* (the Nourisher) and *al-Fattah* (the Opener) had. Working with these Names created a sense of being nourished and open.

Along the way there are lots of ways to reflect on it and talk about it, but at the end the simplicity of it comes back to *La illah illa Allah*. It is enough for us to be in that state, witnessing everything, and still there's nothing but your inner state.

With the constant repetition of the Divine Names, you become more intelligent because the Divine Intelligence is working things out for you every step of the way. Your knowing is immediate and instantaneous.

The Divine takes care of a lot of things for the one who has really entrusted himself or herself to the Divine through the practice of remembrance. The Divine allows you to know things without a lot of the processes that you formerly relied upon. Through this work with the Name you more easily accept not knowing.

So we have traveled through the concepts of principle, language, Divine Names, all the way to the idea of simple presence beyond thought. One who learns to use language and thought consciously is one who thinks more clearly yet is not enslaved by thought. One who learns to enter the reality of the Divine Name moves beyond language as label and enters the qualitative experience of the Divine Name. In truth, all the Divine Names are aspects of our own being, latent within our humanity, waiting to be discovered, activated, and skillfully expressed.

Beauty as a Way of Life

BEAUTY is our point of contact with Love. Beauty has been created for a purpose. It touches us and awakens something in our own faculties. We respond with love.

Within the Mevlevi tradition, beauty is developed as a way of life. There is beauty in its art, music, literature, food, and architecture. This art of extraordinary beauty comes alive in community. Sufism is more "community" than "tutorial." The ideal Sufi community has an energy of beauty and love.

Beauty and love can radiate from the human face. Epiphany is held with the face because the face has the potential of shining forth the Divine. Islam does not encourage representational art in the sacred context. Nevertheless, Bektashi Sufis used calligraphy to fashion faces out of words as an appreciation and recognition of the human face's potential to radiate the Divine.

The idea of reflecting beauty in the mirror of action takes us a little further than just being a passive witness of beauty. It is advising us to internalize beauty and, in turn, lovingly express beauty in our action. Beauty is our point of contact with Love. In this poem from *The Drop That Became The Sea*, Yunus Emre speaks of this kind of beauty.

> To be in love with Love is to gain a Soul,
> to sit on the throne of hearts.
> To love the world is to be afflicted,
> later the Secrets start to make sense.
> Don't be a bramble,
> become the rose.
> Let your maturity unfold,
> the brambles will only burn.
> Prayer was created by God so man could ask for help.
> It's too bad if you have not learned to ask.

The Word and the Name

Accept the breath of those who are mature,
let it become your divining rod.
If you obey yourself, things turn out wrong.
Renouncing the world is the beginning of worship.
If you are a believer, believe this.
Respect your parents and ancestry,
and you will have fine green clothes of your own.
If you earn the complaints of neighbors,
you'll stay in Hell forever.
Yunus heard these words from the Masters.
If you need this advice take it.
They say one who is received by a mature heart
becomes more beautiful.

Sustaining Progress on the Path

WE DON'T NEED TO BE A MYSTIC to know that time is moving fast. However, there is only "now." Our possibilities are accelerated and our responsibilities are greater. The need for healing is greater for those who can heal and hold everything with equanimity.

We are individuals and a group who have reached some level of maturity, sincerity, and understanding. We have developed the capacity for some inner clarity and emptiness. Our ability to come to a point of stillness and equanimity has grown. We have worked to expand our capacity to connect with this Divine Spirit and Source of Mercy. What do we see is required in the time in which we live? Where may our work and responsibility lie?

Maybe we thought when we entered on our journey it was all about working out our own psychological knots, traumas, and wounds. Yes, that too is included in our work. However, that can't be our exclusive or primary focus. Those things will be healed better through service. The false self will evaporate in the sunlight of Reality because it's unreal anyway. If we just stop fortifying it, it'll pass and the Real will remain. The I-ness without "I" will be there in the moment we are capable of holding all of this in the space of our own hearts with consciousness, with love, with remembrance of God.

There is in that inner and infinite space of our own heart a huge possibility and a responsibility for healing every relationship we're involved with. We can do this by holding every relationship in a positive light, with tenderness and with respect. This should especially include the difficult ones. We hold the world with all of its conflict and ignorance in that inner space. We can constantly do the work of healing a personal relationship by noticing every judgment that comes up within us. We can then neutralize and transform the judgment with love. Everything that comes within our own heart consciousness is there for us to work with and heal. This includes the healing of the world. Judgment is not the same as discernment. *Discernment* is "perception" while *judgment* is "blaming."

Mevlana's *Masnavi* is concerned with the subject of union with God. Book Five is really the book of enlightenment. The first lessons we are given are about service, curbing the ego, generosity, and respect. Book Five begins with a story of four birds based on a *hadith* where the Prophet says we have to deal with a duck, a rooster, a crow, and a peacock. The duck is desire and gluttony. The rooster is lust. The peacock is pride and the crow is worldliness. Worldliness refers to wanting more and more as well as chasing after something else that seems better than what we have. It refers to getting sucked into the ambitions that worldliness stimulates in us. The duck, meanwhile, is always putting something in its mouth. It is constantly digging in the ground, relentlessly looking for more and more and more. Similarly we have the metaphorical attributes of the rooster, the peacock, and the crow. This is where we begin. Mevlana says we have to deal with these four things.

A related quote in Book Five comes from a very interesting *hadith,* in which the Prophet says, "The person of faith eats with one stomach and the unbeliever eats with seven stomachs."

What is a "person of faith" and who is "the one in denial?" It was known and recognized that when people become imbued with Spirit that their appetites lessened. This, in turn, refers to a story when the Prophet received some guests. He provided rooms for them in his house. The guests were people who had no spirituality. The story says that when they sat to eat with the Prophet, they ate vast amounts of everything that was served. One of the guests ate so much that, when he went back to the room that he had been given to stay in, he could not control his bowels. This man was extremely ashamed of himself for his behavior and the consequences. The Prophet somehow distracted the man, went into the man's room and cleaned up the mess himself. The Prophet took great and discrete care to resolve all the consequences of the faux pas in such a way that this man's honor was preserved. It is an example of the incredible mercy we may receive.

Some of these teachings from the *Masnavi* may already be familiar to us. But in Book Five, Mevlana also makes a statement about *shariah*, *tariqah*, and *Haqiqah*. *Shariah* can be translated as "the Law," *tariqah* as "the Path," and *Haqiqah* as "the Reality." What he says is quite controversial. A lot of people, including Sufis, might argue with what he says. Mevlana says, "*Shariah* is knowledge" and describes *shariah* as a candle with its purpose being to guide you to the Path. Mevlana says that once you are on the Path you are under *tariqah*, which is "work and action." *Tariqah* leads to the realization of *Haqiqah*. Once we have known *Haqiqah* (Reality) we do not need the "candle of *shariah*" which had guided us to that realization. It does not mean that the morals are transcended, but now one is able to live the realization, to apply and practice it in one's life.

In recent times *shariah* has received a bad name because of its distortion and misuse by certain people. *Shariah* is not really to blame. The Ten Commandments are essentially *shariah* relating to morality, virtue, social justice, and human rights. *Shariah* is not to be understood as something to be frightened of, even if someone somewhere exercises it without mercy or in a narrow and distorted way. *Shariah* has a long, rich, beautiful, and generous history within Islam. It certainly has much for us to learn from.

Wayfaring on the Path has its own principles, customs, and guidelines. The *tariqah* is designed to lead us to *Haqiqah* which comes from *Haqq*, the Truth; the real *Haqiqah* is the state of one who has passed away from the false self and has come to what Mevlana says is I-ness with no "I." Mevlana says that for those who have attained the state of *Haqiqah*, *shariah* is not necessary and you do not even need *tariqah*.

Towards the end of Book Five comes a profound description of selflessness. It is in the words of Ayaz, the wonderful slave of a Sultan. Ayaz asks for forgiveness on behalf of a group of sinners. He says to the Sultan, "You are the most generous. You are the most forgiving. All bounty comes from you. If you don't forgive them, who is going to forgive them?" Ayaz makes this wonderful plea but is then reprimanded for thinking that he could be an intercessor for these people given that he himself is a slave. The forgiveness is not withheld but Ayaz is put in his place. With this, he realizes that the prayer of forgiveness for the sinners could not have come from himself. It could come only from God. Ayaz says:

> Since this house has been emptied of my furniture,
> nothing wet or dry in the house belongs to me.
> You have caused prayer to flow like water from me:
> now make my prayer real and let it be granted.

[*Masnavi* V, 4161–62]

Book Five ends with Ayaz saying,

> Maybe these drunkards broke Your cup,
> and yet those intoxicated by You should be excused.
> The Law does not punish the drunk until they are sober,
> but will I ever become sober again?
> Whoever has drunk from your cup,
> is free of self-consciousness and penalties.
> Your Grace is saying to our hearts,
> "You who have fallen like a gnat
> into the buttermilk of My Love,
> you are not intoxicated,
> you are the Wine Itself."

[*Masnavi* V, 4198, 4202–07]

This is all part of a coherent metaphysics of generosity, forgiveness, oneness, and extraordinary beauty.

> It was Your Mercy, O Self-Subsisting Living One,
> that said, "I created creatures

that they might profit from Me,
not that I might profit from them."
By Your Generosity all defected things are made whole.
Pardon these body-worshipping slaves.
"As exiles in the world you suffered like strangers:
so that you might learn to value Me, O Noble Souls.
Now stretch out your legs in the intoxication
of delight beneath the shade of My tree.
Stretch your legs, rest forever
in these hands and on these bosoms,
while your heavenly companions say,
'These Sufis have returned from their travels.
Sufis as pure as sunlight who for so long had fallen in filth,
have returned undefiled without a stain
as the sunlight to the lofty orb.'"

[*Masnavi* V, 4173–75, 4183–88]

But he did not stop with that. In the end even the sinners themselves say, "We want to be in the ranks of prayer too. Purify us so that we can stand with those who worship."

Aware of their faults and sins,
defeated by a throw of Your dice.
They now want to wash themselves clean
and stand in the ranks of the purified....
It was then that the pen broke and the paper tore.
Did any cup ever measure the sea?
or any lamb carry off a lion?
If you are veiled, step through the veil
and see this Amazing Sovereignty.

The mountains are drunk with You,
the compass and where it points are in Your Hands.
The torment that makes some tremble is trembling at You,
and every precious pearl is cheap compared to You.

[*Masnavi* V, 4190, 4193, 4195–97, 4209–10]

Kabir Helminski is a translator of the works of Rumi and others, a Shaikh of the Mevlevi Order (which traces back to Jalaluddin Rumi), co-director of The Threshold Society (Sufism.org) and Director & Founder of the Baraka Institute (barakainstitute.org). From 2000-2010 he was co-director of the Book Foundation (TheBook.org) publishing the work of Muhamad Asad and developing a series of ground-breaking books on Islamic education. In 2009 Kabir was named as one of the "500 Most Influential Muslims in the World" by Georgetown University and the Royal Strategic Studies Center (Jordan). He has toured North America as Shaikh with the Whirling Dervishes of Turkey bringing Sufi culture to more than 100,000 people in universities, performing arts centers, and cathedrals.

The focus of his work has been developing an "applied spirituality," based in classical Sufism, that can meet the needs of our time. The Threshold Society offers spiritual training to small groups throughout North America, the UK, the Netherlands, Pakistan, Turkey, and Indonesia.

As part of this he has also focused on issues of translation of spiritual concepts from Arabic and other Islamic languages into contemporary English. *The Book of Language* (The Book Foundation) contributes to a new language of spirituality to express the fundamental psychological and metaphysical truths of the spiritual process.

He has written for The Huffington Post, Patheos.com, Tikkun, and The Times of India.

His books on spirituality, *Living Presence* and *The Knowing Heart*, have been published in at least eight languages. In 2017 *Living Presence* was published in a commemorative 25th anniversary edition in the Spiritual Cornerstones series by Penguin Books. Among his recent publications are: *Love's Ripening, Rumi on the Heart's Journey* (Shambhala 2010); *The Rumi Daybook* (Shambhala 2012), and *Holistic Islam: Sufism, Transformation, and The Needs of Our Time* (Threshold Books).

www.ingramcontent.com/pod-product-compliance
Lightning Source LLC
LaVergne TN
LVHW011829060526
838200LV00053B/3954